The 180 Degree Wellness Revolution

Simple Steps
To Prevent and Reverse Illness

TARA L. GESLING, CHHC

Important Notice: The information, ideas, and suggestions in this book are not intended as a substitute for professional medical advice or to replace recommendations or advice from physicians or other healthcare providers. This book is sold with the understanding that the author and publisher are not engaged in rendering medical, health, psychological, or any other kind of personal professional services in the book. Rather, it is intended and provided strictly for educational and informational purposes only to help you make informed decisions about your health and to cooperate with your healthcare provider in a joint quest for optimal wellness. If you suspect you have a medical problem, please seek medical attention from a competent healthcare provider.

Before following any suggestions contained in this book, you should consult your primary health provider. Contents of this book and any accompanying material must not, under any circumstances, be construed to have intended to replace, modify or effect in any manner whatsoever the treatment prescribed by your physician. The author and publisher specifically disclaim all responsibility for any liability, loss, damage or risk, personal or otherwise, that is incurred as a consequence, directly or indirectly, of the use and application of the contents of this book.

Because of the dynamic nature of the Internet, any Web addresses or links contained in this book may have changed since publication and may no longer be valid. The views expressed and the information contained in this book are those of the author and are a result of experience and research, or from other resources referenced in this book. Neither the author nor the publisher have any control over and do not assume any responsibility for third-party web sites or their content.

By reading this book or using any contents from this book or any accompanying material, all readers thereby EXPRESSLY agree and warrant that all actions taken pursuant to and results arising from the reading or use of any of this book's contents or viewing of associated videos or material are their own acts and they bear the sole responsibility and accept the full consequences of their own actions, holding the author totally harmless and free of an liability. Furthermore, by reading this book, the reader agrees that the contents of this book and accompanying material do not provide advice, diagnosis, treatment, or cure for any disease process.

Library of Congress Control Number: 2014953866

ISBN: 978-0-9908806-8-4

DEDICATION

To my daughter and my husband. Thank you for the encouragement and for believing I indeed had a book inside me waiting to be written!

To Jyl, my close friend, who first opened my eyes to the possibility of healing.

To Dave, Glen and Kathleen. Your support helped get me through some extremely tough days. Thank you for looking out for me.

To all of the people who are experiencing chronic illness, there are so many of you. This book is for you.

I also send out my gratitude to all of the people who have helped me along the way. You are my angels. My deepest appreciation is yours.

CONTENTS

FOREWORD BY SHARYN WYNTERS

As a young actress in my 20s I was diagnosed with cancer. In those days, cancer was not as common as it is now and doctors could not offer me a cocktail of chemotherapy, radiation and surgery. They told me there was little they could do. Ultimately, I decided to take my circumstances in my own hands. What I discovered led me to vibrant health and to a new focus in life. Today, as a naturopath, I understand the myriad of ways health is undermined by toxins and chemicals in the environment, by food refining and processing, by commercial farming practices, by stresses that result from thought patterns, and by a culture that has come to rely on quick fixes (pills) rather than finding the root cause of our problems.

Tara Gesling's experience is similar to my own in many ways. Her downward spiral into reflex sympathetic dystrophy (RSD), arthritis, thyroid disease, chronic fatigue syndrome and fibromyalgia, left her in a wheelchair with no hope of recovery. However, Tara's near death experience made it very clear to her that her diet, her lifestyle and her conditioning to follow established medical practices were compounding her symptoms. Tara got a second chance to learn responsibility for her health.

Her research and new choices contributed to her recovery.

The 180 Degree Wellness Revolution includes the story of Tara's return to health. Not only is it deeply inspirational, but it contains a goldmine of information gathered on her journey back to vibrant living. While cancer, heart disease, diabetes, fibromyalgia, and other common conditions have become epidemic, most (if not all) stem from deeper issues that are equally common yet unrecognized by modern medical science. *The 180 Degree Wellness Revolution* gets right to the heart of the issues. It provides the background, the research, and the motivation that can place anyone on a path to prevention and recovery. But best of all, the reader will know they can do it too! As suggested in the subtitle: *Simple Steps To Prevent and Reverse Illness*, the book outlines simple steps to uncovering and undoing the root cause(s) of ill health. Not surprisingly, it will guide the reader back to a basic lifestyle and dietary principles.

Much of what I do as a naturopath is about educating those who come for assistance. *The 180 Degree Wellness Revolution* is a foundational work for providing education and the incentive to change. As a free society, we have choices. However, those choices are often made in ignorance–without complete or accurate information. The act of choosing is often tainted by those who may not have our best interests at heart. *The 180 Degree Wellness Revolution* brings much needed awareness and education to the table.

As Tara says, change begins with a decision. Then, it requires dedication and commitment. Especially in our day when processed and refined foods are so easy; when we have been conditioned to believe pills will take care of everything that ails us, the decision to change can be difficult. *The 180 Degree Wellness Revolution* makes that decision much easier – a no-brainer. I sincerely hope each reader will take advantage of the years of research Tara Gesling has devoted to the wellness revolution and make the decision for a more healthy life.

Sharyn Wynters is an author and naturopath. She is an advocate of whole food nutrition and toxin-free living. Her latest book, The Pure Cure: A Complete Guide to Freeing Your Life From Dangerous Toxins delves into the dangers of the toxins in your modern living environment and how to avoid them.

HOW TO USE THIS BOOK

Have you been taught to believe a diagnosis of illness is inevitably the end of the line? Have you been told, "We don't know what is causing your illness, but we have a pill you can take for a lifetime."? Do you believe all food is the same and has little or no affect on health? Do you wonder why so many people are sick? If you are serious about improving your health and reversing or preventing chronic illness, then this book is for you.

It's time to reverse the current trend of chronic illness, skyrocketing insurance and continual medical bills. We need to do a 180 Degree turn around. Let's create an epidemic of wellness! People are struggling with preventable diseases every day and life shouldn't have to be so difficult. We can reverse this trend by understanding what the causes may be and learning how to prevent illness and maintain health.

I will share with you my personal experience learned while walking through illness. If I repeat certain phrases and concepts throughout this book please know it is intentional and meant to emphasize its importance. Some or all of this information may be new to you. If you feel resistance, try to set it aside and read "with a child's eyes". Children tend to be open and ready to learn new ideas and accept new opportunities. Imagine yourself in this way, wondering where each chapter will lead and what new possibilities may lie ahead. Be prepared to be open to discovery and when you do feel resistance, welcome it and let it pass just as clouds in the sky pass by us every day.

Change begins with a decision. So if you're ready, start there now. If you're not ready at this moment, that's okay too. Simply be open, and set your intentions and future goals. I encourage you to question and research everything. A revolutionary shift in your health and well-being requires dedication and commitment. This is not about willpower though. There is no blame and shame. Instead, it's about building health and learning how to find and heal the root cause of an illness, thus empowering yourself to have an extraordinary life.

INTRODUCTION

Like many Americans, I grew up eating mostly processed fast food. It's called the Standard American Diet (SAD). I had no idea that eating this way could affect my health. Seriously, I didn't! I was a Mountain Dew and Pepsi-holic who could not fathom going a day without soda and M&M's! I celebrated my 30th birthday in a wheelchair wondering why my body was no longer thriving. I mistakenly thought there was nothing I could do about it! Diagnosis and labels included reflex sympathetic dystrophy, fibromyalgia, chronic fatigue, hypothyroid, autoimmune Hashimoto's thyroid disease, arthritis, tinnitus, hypoglycemia, insulin resistance, and high cholesterol, along with a few other things. During the next couple of years I put on over 70 pounds, developed a boat load of allergies and food sensitivities, dealt with extremely debilitating pain, foggy brain, poor memory and had a near death experience before being able to start reversing symptoms. Reverse symptoms? Yes, reverse symptoms! I got rid of 70 pounds. I reversed autoimmune hypothyroidism and rheumatoid arthritis. Blood sugar issues were stabilized and food sensitivities reduced. My body restored nerves and I eventually regained the ability to walk. I burned the cane and gave the wheelchair away. Years later, I was blessed to give birth to a beautiful, healthy baby girl. How did I do this? By digging deep to find courage to face the uncertainty of life along with trusting the brain and gut instincts God gave me.

This book has been written to provide the resources that I wish I could have had over the past 20 years. We are in serious trouble when it comes to health and I want to motivate others to create a movement towards preventive healthcare. The food, agricultural, and medical systems are not designed to help us stay healthy; they are doing quite the opposite. A *180 Degree Wellness Revolution* is necessary if we want to lower health care costs, reduce chronic illness, thrive as we age gracefully and once again give our babies a healthy start. A complete reversal (hence the "180 Degrees") of the direction of the path we are on as a society, is imperative. The current direction of our medical system is not sustainable. Our healthcare system is based on sick care instead of preventive care and has become enormously expensive and disabling to all of us. Insurance, that once cost $25 a month for a family of five, can now cost thousands. We have allowed poor health to become commonplace. It is time to step away from the denial and acknowledge that something is seriously wrong. It is time to educate ourselves and support each other to make real actionable changes. We need to start telling ourselves the truth so we can enjoy life with less confusion and fear.

I have compiled the necessary information along with my experiences, to provide simple steps to prevent illness and reverse disease when possible. I will assist you in identifying what your optimum health and wellness could be. I am not including fluff or information that is readily available elsewhere. I will share with you powerful information I learned on my journey. This is a path you don't have to walk alone. You will learn how to build a support team around you, making rough days easier. You will also learn how to ask the right questions. Illness can sometimes make you feel stranded and alone, like you're on the bank of a rushing river with no crossing. You will find the stepping-stones needed to allow you to cross the river with relative ease. There are many opportunities for healing and bringing quality back into our lives. We need to know how to access and implement them.

My goal is to help you to feel comfortable in your ability to take charge of your health care decisions. You do have a choice in the kind of care you receive based on the training of the practitioners you choose! You can save time, money and regain your quality of life with less effort by understanding that not all practitioners are equally trained or skilled. I want to inspire you to set up an easily attainable plan for maintaining wellness and preventing illness and disease in the future. We are all different and what optimum health is for one person may not be the same for another. The human body is amazingly resilient, it's designed to adapt and heal.

Thank you for choosing the *180 Degree Wellness Revolution* as your guide to a healthier you. I truly hope it challenges and assists you and your loved ones in attaining a new level of health awareness and wellness with ease. Now, let's get started!

1
WHAT'S GOING ON?

"He who has health has hope and he who has hope has everything"
- Arabian proverb

Being born with the gift of being mechanically inclined has always led me to fix what is broken and not working well. It comes naturally to me and I love doing it. I grew up repairing and working on cars and tractors. Rebuilding a motor was fun for me! As I got older I attended college classes in auto mechanics. A few years later, when I became ill, I naturally began comparing my body to that of a car, or the logic used when one is trying to figure out why a car isn't functioning well. That may sound silly to some people, but I grew up with a fascination and curiosity of how things worked. This fascination has served me well.

Humor me for a moment and let's look at how my perspective works. Think about what happens when your car breaks down. First, you take the car to a mechanic to have it looked at. The mechanic would perform a physical and computerized diagnostic assessment. Utilizing both, the mechanic looks for what is malfunctioning and causing the symptoms. After finding the root cause of the problem, your car is then fixed and you go home with a car that is running optimally. Makes sense, right? What would you think if the mechanic didn't repair your car, but instead said to you, "Your car's oil pressure is too high and we must lower the pressure before it ruins your engine. Instead of investigating the cause, I will give you a pill that can be added to the oil once a day to thin and reduce the thickness, which will reduce the pressure. Let me know if you notice any side effects which could cause additional damage. Don't forget to add the pill every day or you'll risk blowing that engine! You'll need to buy these pills every month for the rest of the car's life. Sorry about the extra expense. Have a good day now."

Would you be willing to spend money every month for pills to thin oil or would you look at this person like he's crazy as you leave to take your car to another mechanic? I know I would go to a mechanic who will figure out the cause of the rise in oil pressure and fix the problem before it escalates into a more serious issue. This is safer and will save me a lot of money and aggravation in the long run.

What if your blood pressure was the problem instead of the car's oil pressure? Are you going to take a pill for the rest of your life or are you going to find a practitioner who will find what's causing your blood pressure to be abnormally high? Do you see a problem here? You wouldn't accept a mechanic treating you or your car in this manner but you might accept a doctor doing so. This was basically what doctors were doing with me and it didn't make sense. I had a tough time understanding their logic and thankfully, I eventually followed my gut instead of that logic.

There is a realization slowly rising in our society that the balance is off and problems abound in this model we call health care. People wake every day barely able to drag themselves out of bed and somehow convince themselves that it's okay and they are healthy. Children are being plagued with ear infections, allergies, autism and cancers. When I was a kid it was unheard of for a child to have cancer. Schools didn't have to worry about children with severe allergies because it was so rare. Why is there such denial today about what is going on right in front of our very own eyes? Why are we not being truthful with ourselves? Does a truly healthy person really have to drag themselves out of bed every morning and consume pills for blood pressure, headaches, cholesterol, hormones and arthritis to get through a day? Really? No, I don't think so.

Seventy years ago, what was the percentage of people with high blood pressure, allergies, rheumatoid arthritis, heart disease, diabetes, MS, lupus, thyroid disease, and so on? What were the odds of having cancer or autism 70 years ago? Most autoimmune and chronic diseases were very rare 70 years ago. What has changed? Why is sickness and lack of wellness considered normal? It's common now, but it's NOT normal. We have been taught to accept illness and disease as normal in our hurried, stressed lives. Why do so many doctors prescribe synthetic drugs like they are candy? Is your body somehow lacking in synthetic acid blockers, ACE inhibitors, beta-blockers, calcium channel blockers and vasodilators? These synthetic drugs were not utilized by the human body prior to the last 60 or so years ago, so what's going on? Is it a lack of drugs or a lack of nutrients that's causing so much trouble in our bodies?

Let's look at the word "disease" and break it down into its true meaning. "Dis" means lack of. "Ease" means a comfortable state free from worries, a lack of difficulty. So the word "dis-ease" means the body is functioning with a *lack of ease*. Think about that for a moment and how it could apply to you. I now think of my body in terms of how I want it to function with ease. Doesn't that sound better? Is it possible to reverse dis-ease? Not always, but certainly it is possible in many cases.

I have been blessed to live on farms and care for animals most of my life. I've observed much over the years and I know that nutrition is the most important factor in keeping farm animals healthy and happy and in keeping the veterinarian out of my bank account. On the rare occasion one of my animals is not feeling well, the first thing I do is observe its body condition and look at the stool to see what it may tell me. I then gather a fecal sample for the veterinarian to examine the stool! This is standard practice; the veterinarian knows to look for signs of parasites, infections, nutritional deficiencies, and other possible root causes in his or her patient. Why are most medical doctors not looking at this valuable information to help human patients? Have you ever given a fecal (stool) sample during a medical exam? I know I never did until a few years ago. Doctors laughed at me when I asked them if they do fecal testing. The information I eventually attained from this testing was vital to my regaining health.

Often, conventional medicine does not search for or treat underlying conditions of illness. Most doctors are not trained to think that way anymore. They no longer seem to get curious. It appears they've been trained to diagnose symptoms and prescribe a pharmaceutical pill. They're not asking "why" there is a problem in the first place. They aren't asking themselves what might be malfunctioning and causing the symptom. Spending valuable time with a patient and utilizing a whole person approach to get an idea of what's going on seems to take a backseat to a five minute visit and lab diagnosis. How can a doctor assess a patient's condition in just a few minutes? Medicine hasn't always been practiced this way!

As patients, we are conditioned to believe there's a magic pill for every illness and not to pay close attention to ingredients and possible side effects of medications. People are being told it's normal to be tired all the time. We're told it's part of getting older. We're told that because it's common today, it's normal. I disagree. I've known many people in their 60's, 70's and 80's who were thriving! There is so much poor health in our world today it seems we don't even realize it's not normal to be sick and sluggish.

How have things changed over the past 70 years? How did this nation become the home of so many sickly people? What is out of balance? What's different about our food? Why is it perfectly acceptable for farmers to spray plants that will be eaten as food with neurotoxic poisons? Why would they think we won't absorb the poisons or be affected by it? Most food in grocery stores is highly processed, full of preservatives and loaded with chemicals. Do we really think we can strip and process most nutrients out of food and put synthetic chemicals in their place, with no adverse effects? What would happen to your car if you did the same thing with its fuel? Not only would your car's motor not run, but it would probably damage most of the internal parts not designed to handle contact with those types of chemicals. Replacing car engine parts is relatively easy, although expensive. Not necessarily the case for human body parts.

How has our toxin load changed? Do we all have the same ability to remove and detox the toxins? What about bio-Individuality (each person is unique and has individualized nutritional requirements)? Does a "one-size-fits-all" paradigm really work? Why does dieting feel like a rough ride on a rollercoaster? Are you really unable to lose weight because you're lazy and don't diet enough, or could it be because something else is causing it? Does emotional trauma really affect our health? These are some of the questions I have had to ask myself over the years. I don't have all of the answers, but I do have a much better understanding from my own experiences, many years of research and working with others.

I want to encourage you to ask some of these very important questions of yourself. Use the information in this book to explore and find answers that are true for you. I came to the realization many years ago that to heal this amazing body I was blessed with, I must first understand the root cause of the illness affecting it. I believe our bodies are designed to heal under most circumstances. I found that I was unknowingly getting in the way of my body healing. I had been participating in creating an environment where illness could not only survive, but thrive. Not on purpose! I simply didn't know. Nor did I have any idea of the consequences of the daily choices I was making. These daily choices included: food, habits, household products, stress, relationships and communication. I had to re-think my actions and realize what I was participating in and creating. How could I possibly be creating any of this? Well think about it... everything must have some kind of food to survive, and that includes chronic illness and disease. I had to figure out how I might be participating in feeding it and then take steps to change it... No blame, no shame. I'll say that one more time — NO BLAME, NO SHAME. Rethinking our actions is not necessarily about right or wrong, or putting our past under a microscope. It's about learning what we've been doing that doesn't feed and nourish our soul. It's about being really honest within, and to allow and promote healing throughout.

A healthy body functions 100% as it was designed to. You don't have to train your cells to do their job because they already know what to do. Our goal is to have 100% function, which is normal. When the body is fully functioning, it is in a state of ease and you are healthy. When the body is not fully functioning, ease has been disrupted or imbalanced and dis-ease exists. Symptoms are the last stage of dis-ease.

Prior to the appearance of symptoms, changes take place in the body, and these changes result in symptoms. I understand symptoms are not typically thought of in this way, but think about it for a moment. By the time symptoms show up, the imbalance causing them has been going on for a while. An example of such a case is endometriosis or uterine fibroids. I know a number of women dealing with these types of illnesses. Why aren't doctors investigating what might be causing the endometriosis or fibroids? What balance is off in the body that allows for the growth of endometriosis or fibroids? What is feeding it? It may be common these days, but it's not normal. Symptoms are a signal that something is wrong. Because symptoms are common we are frequently told they are normal. No symptom is normal. When a previously healthy person begins showing symptoms of illness, something isn't functioning properly. A balance is off. The body is unable to adapt to whatever the stressors are. The question of "why" should be asked! Stressors can be physical, emotional, mental, structural, environmental or chemical. When a malfunction has occurred, it's vital to find out what the stressors are to regain functional health. In today's world this can be tricky without the right guidance. I know from personal experience.

I spent the past 25 years working with various practitioners, researching and being my own health detective with the goal of regaining a healthy body. It has been challenging and immensely frustrating on many days but immeasurably rewarding on others. Many times I came close to giving up, because I felt hopeless. Several times I would start getting better only to have another setback. Through it all, I have been able to improve my health, confidence and well-being. I found courage I never realized I had. I became empowered and learned I can accomplish just about anything I set my mind to. I've gained so much respect for the awesome design of the human body and its ability to heal.

We are at a critical time in this country especially when it comes to our health. We must wake up from our sleepy denial and see how unhealthy and misled we've become as a nation. Ask yourself the following questions:

- Do you wake up feeling exhausted and disappointed you didn't get a restful sleep?
- Do you wonder whether you'll ever sleep restfully again and not struggle to get going in the morning?
- Are you tired of dieting and hearing experts say it's because you're lazy and don't diet enough that you can't lose weight and keep it off?
- When you brush your teeth do you recognize the tired, puffy face staring at you in the mirror?
- Is your hair thinning or falling out?
- Do you have dark circles under your eyes and more lines on your face than are on your child's notebook paper?
- Do you or your child get ear, chest or throat infections or have allergies frequently?
- Do you find yourself feeling stuck, hopeless or fearful of a body that just doesn't seem to want to cooperate with you?
- Do you wonder how you got this way?
- Have you been diagnosed with a disease or autoimmune condition?
- Do you find yourself getting more and more confused about what is healthy and what is not?
- Does the thought of getting older and continuing down this road scare the heck out of you?

- Do you wonder whether there is anything that will help you turn your health around for the better?

If you answered yes to any of these questions, you're not alone. Learning how to create simple, 'do-able' healthy habits is crucial. With simple steps, you can create a lifestyle that is easier, reduces stress and will enable you to feel like a new person. Are you ready to empower yourself and find a new level of awareness about your own ability to heal? Are you ready to get off of the diet roller coaster that makes you feel like a failure? Are you ready to start enjoying delicious food that actually promotes health? Are you ready to join the *180 Degree Wellness Revolution* and motivate others to do the same?

2
THE STORY OF ME

Look reality square in the eye. When you refuse to back away from it, you are living in courage.

I know what it's like to feel sick for a very long time with no cure on the horizon. I spent my teen years being active, living on a farm, driving a tractor, learning a bit about gardens and growing a few veggies. I had the same typical illness as most of my friends; the common cold, flu viruses and strep throat. And I did everything that everyone else did – took antibiotics and would get better. I began working when I was old enough and loved having the ability to be independent. I moved out on my own and had no clue of the road ahead of me.

I thought I was in good health at the age of 27, I really did! I was married and happy with life. My husband and I bought an abandoned small farm that needed a lot of renovating. It was so exciting and I looked forward to beginning every day in the country with the sights and smells I grew up with and adore.

We were heading into the fall season; the leaves on the trees were just starting to turn shades of yellow, red, and brown. I peered through my kitchen window watching the sun rising above the 40 foot pine trees in the back yard and thinking it was going to be a fabulous day. Ideas were bouncing through my mind as I headed out the back door to the barn. The horses were lined up along the fence awaiting my arrival. I was halfway there and suddenly felt an odd sensation. It was an unfamiliar feeling. I didn't recognize the significance until I found myself without balance. I fell to the ground in what seemed like slow motion. My legs and sense of balance were gone. As I lay on the ground dazed and confused, I surveyed what had happened and thought I must have tripped. I pulled myself together, wiped the grass off my knees, and got up to continue the walk to the barn.

Due to an injury to my left leg that was terribly slow in healing, the daily walk to the barn had been my main exercise. The pain and swelling remained after an entire year. This didn't make sense to me. The doctors repeatedly reminded me I needed to be patient because some things take more time to heal. They said it would eventually go away and I needed to keep using and exercising my leg as much as I could tolerate. My parents always said, "The doctor knows best!" and I did as I was told.

As weeks passed I increasingly found myself on the ground confused and dazed. I knew it was time to let go of my denial. I had to admit it wasn't normal. Even when my doctor did not find it alarming, I did. Prior to this, I had always been strong and my balance always good. Heck, I was a majorette and gymnast in high school, and a skilled equestrian! Balance had always been one of my assets. I asked myself repeatedly what could be going on and is it related to my unhealed leg injury. Where do I go for the answers to the questions I asked myself?

The symptoms and pain became more severe. The doctor basically said I was being "overly sensitive". What I didn't realize was the medical doctor had no idea what was happening to my body, much less how to heal it. This moment was the beginning of a lifetime of learning about my amazing body, my strengths, weaknesses, a broken medical system, health and wellness and the not-so-small task of reversing the effects of a neurodegenerative and autoimmune dis-ease.

My life was changing drastically. Actually, let me rephrase that, it was spinning out of control. My body was sending signals no one seemed to be able to explain. My life would depend on my taking full responsibility for my health and well being, yet I had no idea how to do it, much less where to begin. Thank God for small favors, because I had no idea that I would spend the next four-and-a-half-years in a wheelchair.

The Diagnosis

I was frustrated, humiliated, swollen and in pain, repeatedly finding myself on the ground and decided to seek a consultation with an Orthopedic physician outside of my healthcare plan. He then referred me to a doctor who specialized in pain and neuromuscular illness. This doctor recognized the symptoms my body was displaying. The diagnosis I received was advanced stage RSD; reflex sympathetic dystrophy. Additional diagnoses followed within the year. They included autoimmune thyroid disease, arthritis, chronic fatigue and fibromyalgia along with a few others. I was relieved to finally have a label for the symptoms I was dealing with. I had validation my experience was real and actually had a medical name. I later realized the label that came with the diagnosis was anything but good. You will understand more as you read further.

Initially, I needed to understand what RSD was, so I began researching and what I found was beyond frightening. How could this be? I was in a state of shock because this was not how my life was supposed to go! I just wanted to get better and get back to my active life. Autoimmune hypothyroid, fibromyalgia, arthritis and chronic fatigue were the next subjects of study. Keep in mind that this was in the late eighties and there was no Internet. I subscribed to medical journals and books. I read everything I could get my hands on whenever possible.

I was prescribed many medications and I took them faithfully. It was my belief the pills would help to improve my health. I had no clue synthetic medications could negatively impact my body and internal organs causing additional problems. The more I researched the more I came to realize people with these types of conditions, especially advanced stage, aren't expected to be able to return to a normal life. My research suggested I may experience severe permanent disability, brain changes, autonomic nervous system (all the automatic things your body does without you controlling it) and central nervous system issues. Oh my gosh, the reality of what I was living with came crashing down on me like a ton of bricks.

This was the beginning of my long journey. It has taught me enormously. I thank God every day that I'm a very optimistic person by nature. This has helped me to persevere in the toughest of times. To be diagnosed with a horribly painful and crippling disease and to be told the expectations of recovery are slim was mind bending in so many ways. I was only 27! My five-foot-two-inch, small framed body, was designed to be way better than this! As the pain and circulatory problems increased and I continued to lose more use of my leg, I went through the "why me" victim stage which was followed by anger.

By 1990 I was relying on a wheelchair for mobility. I was on a slew of medications that included some heavy duty pain killers. I had gone from being a fully functional, full time working woman who rode horses daily to someone I no longer recognized. I continued to research, but the loss of hope to regain my health became overwhelming to me. The medications affected my memory and this made it hard to retain information.

Near Death Experience

I was ready to just give up as I began to question my own mortality. My weight had increased by a staggering 70 pounds. I could barely function most days. I would look in the mirror but didn't recognize the face staring back at me. I felt trapped and dreadfully alone. In 1993 I decided it was all just too much and began praying God would show me how to heal or take me. I could never consider taking my own life (never!) so it had to be by God's choice. My prayer was eventually answered although a bit differently than I expected. However, a near death experience is not what I was counting on, yet it turned out to be one of the biggest blessings ever.

Unlike many people who experience near death experiences I was not under anesthesia, in surgery or at a terminal point in the illness. I was sitting reclined in a comfy chair in my living room with my husband and close friends watching a movie. I could not have imagined what was going to transpire that evening. I felt my heart stop and moments later left my body. The understanding I came back with changed my life completely.

I was fully aware my heart was no longer beating. I remember not being able to move and wondering when a normal rhythm would re-establish. Suddenly, I found myself looking at the room from a perspective several feet above where my body was sitting. It took a moment to grasp what was going on. I felt weightless and had no form, yet I was still me. The pain I had been feeling was gone! I could not remember ever feeling so good. I was full of joy. I watched as my husband and friends continued viewing a movie, totally oblivious to what was happening to me. I saw my body sitting in the chair unconscious. A moment later I found myself within a beautiful light surrounded by warmth and love. I wasn't afraid at all. I was excited! I was in the presence of a community of others, many of whom I knew and loved. It felt like a reunion. The colors I saw were vibrant and stunning, so much more so than on Earth. Information seemed to flow through me effortlessly. Whatever I needed to know was instantly available. I was happy to be there and there were no concerns or thoughts of going back to my body. I was given an opportunity to view my life on what I refer to as the "big screen". I was comforted and could see things clearly and objectively from this new perspective. I didn't feel judged, I felt thankful and reassured. It reminded me of being "the fly on the wall" of my own life. It was confirmed to me we are not alone, we have angels and guides. We are here to learn and experience love, unconditional love. We are all born with the amazing gift of intuition and we need to use it. **We need to learn to love others and probably more than anything ... ourselves.** It's difficult to love others unconditionally if you don't show yourself unconditional love and understanding.

I came to understand that honesty and truth are necessary ingredients for unconditional love. Loving ourselves includes saying no to putting harmful chemicals and fake foods on our plates and in our bodies. I had to get really honest with myself on the fake processed food issue and it wasn't easy. I literally had to see that I had become addicted to chemicals in foods. I had plenty of excuses I would tell myself such as: "I'm on a budget and other foods are too expensive", "It's too much effort to cook (especially from a wheelchair)," or my best one, "It can't be that bad, I've been eating this stuff my entire life and it hasn't killed me yet!" These were simply beliefs and NOT the truth.

I had to realize certain manufacturers use artificial flavors to make food very rewarding to your taste receptors and pathways in the brain because they are in business to sell food. They want us to come back again and again. They basically hijack reward pathways in the brain to addict us to their foods. I hadn't yet connected the harm from chemicals and processed foods. Quite frankly, I didn't want to because it would mean I would have to make changes. Change, especially at that time in my life, was not easy and I resisted. Up until that day, I was addicted and would use any justification to keep eating the same way. If I wanted inner peace it was mine, but I had to stop defending, pretending, denying and lying to myself. I had to own up and step away from the false perceptions, and surrender.

I understood I needed to stop putting myself down and stop letting others overpower me as if I was not important. Furthermore, I would have to let go of perfection and learn to trust myself. Most inability to love comes from fear. We live in a fear based society! No wonder life can feel so crazy at times. Understanding this will help you to move away from fear and towards love. I specifically recall the words told to me as if they were said yesterday, "Make no decision based on fear." Of course this is not always an easy thing to do, but I do my best.

I knew from that moment on I came to earth to experience what I was experiencing and I was going to be okay. I would have help and those who were to guide me would show up in my life when I was ready for them. I had to be aware of this, recognize the help, and most of all choose to accept it. We ALL have choices. **Choices are based on belief and I had to examine my beliefs** learned from childhood. I had to learn to be honest with myself about relationships, about food and about what was going on in my life every day.

Right before returning to my body, I remember understanding it wasn't my time yet and that I still had things to do. My grandmother (deceased) was telling me "baby steps" and then I heard a song from the Christmas TV special "Santa Claus is

Coming To Town." The lyrics, "Put one foot in front of the other and soon you'll be walking 'cross the floor; put one foot in front of the other, and soon you'll be walking out the door", ushered my return to earth and has stayed with me since. When I feel overwhelmed or stressed I hear that song in my mind and smile knowing my grandmother is still with me. This whole experience reminded me of where my home really is and that we are here for a very short period. I am here, as we all are, with a purpose and a reason. Whatever is in your way, holds you down, or has you paralyzed with fear, fear not. You will prevail. Be truthful with yourself and you won't feel the need to shrink back from anyone or anything.

Following my near death experience, I knew I could heal myself. I wasn't sure of the exact steps I would take, but I knew I could heal. The only odd part for me was the reality of coming back after having received a download of information and insight I didn't quite know what to do with. I knew I would figure it out though. I was no longer afraid of death and I definitely knew angels and God exist. I no longer felt abandoned in this way.

I remember understanding at a very deep level that I was being poisoned by much of the food and medications I had been ingesting for years. I started with what I knew I could change. Changing one thing at a time, baby steps, was one of the keys to my success. I knew my body was overwhelmed and failing and if I was going to survive this, it was up to me to do something about it.

I told my doctor I needed to stop consuming the medications because they were poisoning my body. Some doctors may have looked at me as if I was crazy, but my doctor was an extremely supportive man and I always knew his intentions were to help me in any way he could. He knew I was serious and not crazy. He supported me in the process of the weaning myself off prescription medications over time even though that was his main method of treatment.

I started studying and using herbs to support my body. I slowly went back to growing my own food again and stopped purchasing processed foods with chemical additives. I read about and studied homeopathic medicines. I cooked organic foods whenever possible. A friend of mine, Jyl, would cook extra meals for me when I needed it. This was a really good start and I began to see improvements within six months. Being dependent on a wheelchair and cane made this very challenging, but I loved gardening and I knew this was what I was supposed to do. Scooting around the garden on my butt became one of my favorite activities and I looked forward to doing it all summer long!

One of the hardest and most vital lessons I learned involved not giving my power over to a doctor or anyone else. This is especially hard when you grew up in a family that believed it to be disrespectful to question a doctor. My parents were taught that you do what the doctor tells you, he/she knows better than you. I had to overcome that in order to heal! I had to start questioning everything! We all put our pants on the same way, right? We're all products of what we've been taught until we learn to get curious and think critically and independently. We simply don't know what we don't know. None of us is infallible. The most frightening part of this awareness for me was the 'Oh sh*t moment' when I realized the doctors really had no clue of what to do to help me. Yikes! I cried a lot of tears when I realized there was no magic pill. I don't think I've ever felt so alone. But then, I would remember the near death experience I was blessed with and knew I wasn't all alone and that all would be okay.

I had no idea that in addition to the damage from the synthetic prescription medications, I was also dealing with toxic heavy metals, dental work, pesticides, processed foods, chemicals in personal products, aspartame, and all of the other fake foods and additives I had been eating since I was born. My body was overwhelmed, overburdened, and overtaxed.

I've spent over 20 years implementing and understanding what I learned during that near death experience. What I saw and learned in those moments could be an entire book one day. To put it simply, I've been learning how to stop resisting, while allowing myself to let go, especially letting go of fear. I've been learning how to really trust my God-given instincts, my purpose and the healing ability of my body. I've been learning that healing involves more than just seeing a doctor and taking a pill. I've learned to not take ownership of an illness or its label because I am not the dis-ease; I will not claim it as mine. The symptoms I have dealt with have led me to understand there was a malfunction my body was bringing to my attention. I have had to learn to listen to that communication. As I take notice of the symptoms and action to remove their cause, they can dissolve from my life like clouds passing in the sky. Can all malfunctions be reversed? I don't know. My guess is it will depend on the extent of damage and the ability to remove the cause from your life. For me, this process has taken many years and not all symptoms have gone away because of the extensive damage or inability to remove the cause. I feel as if I've been peeling away layers of an onion over the years. I invested many thousands of dollars into a long line of practitioners and doctors who couldn't tell me what was wrong. I spent so much money with so little result that I felt utterly lost.

As I worked through those years of peeling the onion that was my life, I found each new layer emerged with a teacher capable of guiding me through it. I have to admit it hasn't always been easy and I had to be willing to do the work. It's been quite an adventure. I believe what I have learned and experienced throughout my journey will end up being the future path of preventive nutrition, health, and medicine; the way practitioners will be trained and medicine will be practiced. I'm no guru and I'm definitely not the only person who has experienced this type of revelation. Our medical system has been lost to greed and appears to have been sold out to the highest bidder. Greed and power seems to have become more important than health and happiness. Most of the protocols I have used successfully to reverse illness were practiced long before I was born, yet they are not taught in medical schools today. If a product or procedure can't be patented and hugely profitable, the pharmaceutical corporations seem to do their best to make sure that product or procedure is not readily available or is banned. We've all been deceived, doctors included. Information has been skewed and misinformation has been promoted. People are getting sicker and sicker even as more and more money is spent. Doctors continue to allow their hands to be tied behind their backs and are using prescribed protocols that can harm more than they can heal. We are told the way western medicine is practiced today is superior to all other medicine.

Please don't get me wrong. I have a lot of respect for those trained in the field of medicine. I have many friends who are doctors, and they are truly good people who are frustrated with the way medicine is being practiced. I believe we have the best and worst of both worlds right now. If you're in a car accident or need emergency care, our doctors are probably some of the best trained and many, many lives are saved every day. But when it comes to the backbone of health, preventive medicine, nutrition and wellness, the average doctor is not well informed. Many people are suffering and literally dying very slow, painful deaths. I used to be one of those people and it was a horrible experience. I am grateful for every day that I can roll out of bed and say, "I am not that person literally dying a slow grueling death today."

It makes me shudder to think of what my life would be like right now had I not learned and implemented the changes I have throughout the years. I also feel as if I am the luckiest person alive to have this sense of peace and comfort that I never thought possible.

Let me highlight the good news. I was able to lose 70 pounds and have been able to maintain my pre-illness weight. I have been off of narcotic pain killers and heavy duty meds for approximately nineteen years. The last prescription medication for thyroid was taken approximately 14 years ago.

I'm not advising or advocating you stop taking your prescription medications on your own. I told my doctor I was getting off the meds and asked for his support. It was my personal choice and I took responsibility for it. My doctor and I agreed to continue working together to find ways to help me heal, using methods other than what we had been unsuccessfully employing. I was supporting my body and my nutritional needs through organic, real whole foods, natural supplements and herbs. I was relying on myself, not my doctor to heal.

The status of the dis-eases I was diagnosed and labeled with are honestly unknown in a positive way. I am doing much better now and that is a good thing. I continue to maintain a healthy lifestyle and I teach others how to do the same in a realistic and simple way. I am a Master Gardener, Master Gardener Instructor and am certified in Permaculture. I started teaching workshops on how to garden and farm without chemicals, how to grow healthy, highly mineralized foods, and how to find healthy food if you don't want to grow it. I went back to school and studied sustainable agriculture, nutrition, diet and lifestyle with some of the best teachers in the world including; Joshua Rosenthal,

Deepak Chopra, Dr. Arden Anderson, Neil Kinsey, Dr. Christiane Northrup, Dr. Bernie Siegel, John Douillard, PhD, Dr. Mark Hyman, Debbie Ford, Paul Pitchford, Dr. Andrew Weil. I graduated from the Institute of Integrative Nutrition in New York City. I became certified as a Holistic Health Coach through The State University of New York and the American Association of Drugless Practitioners. I went on to study functional nutrition to become certified as a Functional Diagnostic Nutritionist.

I learned to listen to what my body was telling me and will continue to do this for the rest of my life. Symptoms are the last part of a disease process. I've been able to stabilize and reverse symptoms of many of these dis-eases and labels. However, I am aware of the possibility that if I were to go back to the ways of my old lifestyle, which included a lot of stress and the standard American diet of processed foods and chemicals, things could be different. I have no intention of going back because life today is so much easier, more fulfilling and rewarding than I ever thought possible. This lifestyle works!

3
WHY ARE PEOPLE SO SICK?

I had to learn I had a choice in every moment.

It's fairly easy to get sick in this modern world we live in. Some things we can limit and some we cannot. We have to find a balance because worrying about staying away from all things that stress the body can make you sick too! Some of the biggest contributors are:

- Lack of nutrition
- Poor diet – processed foods and drinks
- Toxic teeth and heavy metals
- Toxic chemicals
- Inflammation
- Emotional and physical stressors
- Toxic relationships
- Genetic expression

If a doctor were to write a prescription to 'easily get sick' it would probably read like this: "Eat a regular diet of processed food, go to bed at 1 am and survive on a few hours of sleep each night, drink fluoridated water and sodas, especially diet sodas and then to finish it all off... allow stress, fear, poor relationships and worry to take prominence in the everyday choices of your life. Yes, it's pretty simple. Does any of this sound familiar in your life? It certainly was present in mine. It's what many of us would call a normal day, but is it really normal? It may be very common, but probably not what we really want as our normal.

A Doctor's Role

So let's first look at the role doctors are currently playing in all of this. Most doctors are not trained in preventive nutrition or how to recognize some of the early signs of illness before things get bad and symptoms show up. I say *most* because I am not including all doctors by any means. I do know of some who are very well trained to recognize and prevent illness and they do a very good job at it. These doctors undergo additional training in functional or integrative medicine to be able to practice at this advanced level. Unfortunately, there are very few of them at this time. So when I speak of most doctors, I am not referring to the doctors with advanced functional and integrative training.

We are in a quandary. It seems most doctors have been taught to treat symptoms, not to search for the actual cause of the symptoms. It appears they are not able to recognize and help their patients prevent the onset of dis-ease when maybe it could be prevented. In other words, from what I've seen and experienced most chronic diseases don't develop overnight. There are changes at the cellular level that take place before symptoms appear. People may feel differently for a while before they're diagnosed with a disease. They may experience changes in sleep pattern, circulation, hair, skin, hormones, blood pressure, blood sugar, memory, cognitive ability, or more. That was my experience for almost two years and the doctors weren't able to help me figure out why I was experiencing these very important changes and symptoms before things got out of control. Nobody looked at my cortisol and hormone levels to see what was happening. Nobody seemed to want to understand why I was experiencing so much pain, swelling and discoloration in my leg. Why? The only answer I can think of is because they apparently didn't know how to. Once there was a diagnosis and we had a name for the collection of symptoms, it was strictly symptom management. What they did do was prescribe pills to try to suppress the symptoms. The pills didn't work and after an extended period of time they caused harm.

In my experience during the first two years prior to a diagnosis, if the pills didn't work, the doctors would get frustrated and try to blame me. They would assume I had not been compliant or I was just a complainer. How many times have you heard of a doctor telling someone it's all in their head or there's nothing wrong? I know I've experienced it. I've learned when they say there is nothing wrong, basically what they are saying is that they don't know what is wrong. There is a big difference between those two statements. Am I knocking doctors? Yes and no, because many times it's a case of "they don't know what they don't know" and they are taught and expected to follow certain protocol. Where I do hold them responsible and will knock away is in their apparent inability or unwillingness to question and recognize a system that isn't working, and doing nothing to change it.

Worse yet, many doctors are supporting this system by putting their heads in the sand and ignoring the problems, even ridiculing or ostracizing the doctors who are trying to actually help patients heal. The doctor who is brave enough to stand up and question the system usually gets picked on and bullied by his peers. Change doesn't come easy. Doctors and other practitioners trying to change things for the better are literally being persecuted for their bravery. This is a very big reason why I believe it's so easy to get sick these days. There is not much support around true preventive care and building health.

Let's go back a few years so you can get a glimpse of what I'm talking about. What is happening today reminds me of what happened to the doctor who is now known as the pioneer of antiseptic procedures. He proposed hands should be washed in between patients and before delivering a baby. His name was Ignaz Semmelweis.[1] Dr. Semmelweis discovered the incidence of puerperal fever could be drastically reduced in obstetrical clinics by simply disinfecting the hands between patients. Puerperal fever was common in the hospital at this time and often fatal, with mortality at 10-35%. Doctor's wards had three times the mortality of midwives wards.[2] His ideas were rejected by the medical community because washing hands was in conflict with the established scientific and medical opinions of that time. Death rates were very high when doctors refused to wash hands and sanitize between patients. Dr. Semmelweis was treated as if he was crazy. He was dismissed from his job and persecuted because he suggested such change. Today, washing hands in between patients or procedures is the standard protocol and you would be told you're crazy and tried for malpractice if you didn't do it. The doctors that are using procedures such as advanced nutrition with cancer patients, dental amalgam removal and heavy metal chelating to help their patients heal are the Dr. Semmelweis's of today.

In my opinion, we have a sick care system not a health care system. Our high health care costs are a reflection of this. Doctors need to stand by their oath to "First Do No Harm" once again. Sick care is very expensive. It is costing ALL of us in so many ways.

Toxic Teeth & Heavy Metals

I am one of the many Americans who had amalgam fillings placed in my teeth when I was a child, and as an adult. I was told it was perfectly safe; yet later found out I had mercury poisoning. According to the EPA web site, *"Dental amalgam, sometimes referred to as 'silver filling', is a silver-colored material used to fill (restore) teeth that have cavities. Dental amalgam is made of two nearly equal parts: liquid mercury and a powder containing silver, tin, copper, zinc and other metals. Amalgam is one of the most commonly used tooth fillings, and is considered to be a safe, sound, and effective treatment for tooth decay."* They go on to say, *"When amalgam fillings are placed in or removed from teeth, they can release a small amount of mercury vapor. Amalgam can also release small amounts of mercury vapor during chewing, and people can absorb these vapors by inhaling or ingesting them. High levels of mercury vapor exposure are associated with adverse effects in the brain and the kidneys."*[3]

Mercury is the second most toxic substance to the human body, and they're saying when it is placed in a tooth and allowed to release gas daily it's safe and sound! The web site goes on to say *"...If amalgam waste is sent to a landfill, the mercury may be released into the groundwater or air. If the mercury is incinerated, mercury may be emitted to the air from the incinerator stacks. And finally, if mercury-contaminated sludge is used as an agricultural fertilizer, some of the mercury used as fertilizer may also evaporate to the atmosphere. Through precipitation, this airborne mercury eventually gets deposited onto water bodies, land and vegetation. Some dentists throw their excess amalgam into special medical waste ("red bag") containers, believing this to be an environmentally safe disposal practice. If waste amalgam solids are improperly disposed in medical red bags, however, the amalgam waste may be incinerated and mercury may be emitted to the air from the incinerator stacks. This airborne mercury is eventually deposited into water bodies and onto land."*

So according to information provided on the EPA web site, when mercury is placed in our teeth it's safe and sound! But, mercury in amalgam is toxic and considered a dangerous contaminant, which must be disposed of as a hazardous waste product when it's everywhere except our teeth. Is the mercury poisoning I've been dealing with safe and sound? Are the mercury tattoos – a dark pigmentation or staining on the gum tissue where an amalgam filling was located – on my gums safe and sound? Saying that small amounts of mercury are safe and sound is about as insane as telling a child who is allergic to peanuts to go ahead and eat just a little. It's safe because it's just a little bit. (Mercury is also present in some vaccines. In addition, mercury is in the new types of fluorescent light bulbs being promoted to the public for use as incandescent bulbs are being phased out.)

Give me a break please. Where is the logic in this? Where is the science? This is daily exposure to an extremely toxic element.

Other Toxic Chemicals

Next, let's look at other toxic chemicals. If you look back seventy or eighty years ago, you'll find there weren't many chemicals in households, gardens, and food. Fluoride wasn't used in public water systems until 1962 and most chemical development took place during the Second World War. If chemicals weren't prevalent eighty years ago, why are they now? Most European countries still refuse to use water fluoridation because of the toxicity. Do the research if you want to be well informed and know what is readily known. Information is plentiful.

Why are there so many chemicals in food today? How are these chemicals affecting your body? Are they slowly contributing to the breakdown of your body? Are they causing damage to your gut and its ability to absorb nutrients and maintain health? Do we really need these chemicals or are they used in place of real food so the industrial food companies can make a higher profit? I don't have a problem with a company making an honest profit, but when it's at the expense of my health I do have a problem with it. If the chemicals are really necessary, why are these companies not using them in food marketed to European countries? Why are the chemicals in our food in the United States, but not in theirs? We are allowing corporations to put chemical poisons in the food we feed our children! Take a look at the ingredient labels of the food you buy. Must we really deprive ourselves of delicious foods to be healthy or do we need to start removing the chemicals? Think about that...there were tons of delicious foods available sixty years ago and most of them were actually good for you. There wasn't an obesity epidemic then that we have now. So, what's different now? Will the new motto for dieting be "fewer chemicals instead of fewer calories?" That's my motto by the way.

Do you ever wonder what effect toxic chemicals have on how sick or healthy society is? Chronic illness was rarely seen years ago, chronic fatigue and fibromyalgia were virtually unheard of. It was not common for someone in your family or friendship circle to have cancer. This has changed drastically. How many people do you know personally that have been touched by cancer? Is there a possibility chemicals in and on our foods, in our air and water, on our lawns and in our personal products could have contributed to this? I think it's possible.

Good health is something we used to think of as a God given right. We're supposed to be born healthy, right? Today, that doesn't seem to happen though, does it? Children today are born with hundreds of chemicals in their blood. The Environmental Working Group (EWG) has a twenty minute documentary that explains this really well. You can find it at *www.ewg.org*. Chemicals, which didn't exist one hundred years ago, are now in the blood of a developing baby! Do you wonder what the effects of this may be? Here are some of the statistics highlighted in the EWG documentary released in 2012: *"...there has been an 84% increase in acute lymphocytic leukemia in children from 1975-2002. There has been a 57% increase in childhood brain cancer. 1 in 150 children now have an Autism spectrum disorder* (and in some locations the numbers are even worse). *Approximately 7.3 million American couples have trouble becoming pregnant or carrying to term, a 20% increase in the last ten years. Sperm counts in men are decreasing approximately 1% per year in the United States. Estimates are now 1 in 3 women will develop cancer and 1 in 2 men will develop cancer in their lifetimes"*.

This is crazy! What is the reason we as a society are allowing this? I say *allowing* because we have not yet said a big collective, really loud NO. Did you know that because of current laws most new chemicals can be approved in just a few weeks and have very few, if any, requirements to be proven safe?

One of the things I've noticed during my lifetime is it appears people are getting sick much earlier than they used to. When I was a kid, as I already mentioned, you rarely ever heard of another kid being sick. You rarely ever heard of a young adult being ill. Most of the older adults of retirement age got along fairly well. I recall people in their 80's still living independently in their own homes and having great memories to share with us. There weren't very many 'old folks homes' because they really weren't needed.

It was usually later in their years when people did get ill, if they got ill at all. Many simply died in their sleep after a long, healthy life. I propose this happened for many reasons; the most important being that they ate real food grown and prepared without chemicals during their childhood development and youth. This allowed the gut microbiome to develop and remain balanced, keeping them healthy. Genetic predisposition was still there, but, the body was able to remain healthy. If they succumbed to illness, it was when they were older and their immune system and gut became more imbalanced. The illness would show up where they were weak or genetically predisposed. The gut microbiome is the ecosystem of bacteria that lives within us. There are at least 100 trillion microbes and bacteria in and on our body and they outnumber cells 10-to-1. Microbes in the gut microbiome perform functions such as digesting food and synthesizing vitamins. They have also been linked to human mood and behavior. If you'd like to research this further, check out the Human Microbiome Project supported by the National Institutes of Health (NIH).

People born in the 1920's may have had their first twenty to forty years without an overload of chemicals stressing their body, depending on where they lived and worked. By the time they would turn seventy or eighty they might show the effects. On the other hand, children born in the 1960's grew up on chemicals. Mothers were advised to feed their babies chemical formulas instead of breast milk, so the proper gut microbiome may have never been established. A baby cow or horse will likely die if it doesn't receive its mother's colostrum! Are we really that different? A lot of babies born in the 1960's are now suffering from chronic illnesses when they are in their prime years! I'm one of them and I was in a wheelchair at 30 years old. I had many friends who were diagnosed with cancers and other autoimmune disease before they turned 40 years old. That used to be unheard of. It seems to me our bodies can only carry these chemicals for so long before breaking down. Now, in the early 2000's there are thousands of chemicals in use and lots of sick children. Is there a connection?

Where are all of the chemicals I speak about? They're in your food, your water and the products you clean your house with. They are sprayed in the air, you wash your hands with them, apply them to your skin, and sleep with them in your bed. They're everywhere!

According to the Environmental Working Group most ingredients used in personal care products are not tested and evaluated for safety. Take a look at the ingredients and if you have concerns about them as I do, simply avoid them as best you can. There are plenty of places to research this information online. The Environmental Working Group has been researching skincare products for more than ten years and has a wonderful database called the "Skin Deep® Cosmetics Database" located on *www.ewg.org*. This site is well researched and credible. Read labels and when you are purchasing, know you are in a buyer beware situation. I personally avoid products with BHA, BHT, parabens, petroleum, phthalates, triclosan, synthetic fragrances, and UV-filtering chemicals.

We have a choice when it comes to personal products. There are companies manufacturing cosmetics and personal care items using ingredients which are not toxic to us. We need to support these companies instead of supporting companies who prefer to use toxic ingredients, choosing higher profits over safety. Vote with your dollars! I choose to use non toxic products and it's so much easier to find them now than it was 15 years ago.

I get a lot of people asking me, "Where can I find cosmetics without harmful chemical ingredients?" I'm happy to say this question is getting easier to answer! I recently became aware of a young company named *Simply Nontoxic Cosmetics.* I have sampled some of their products and am really impressed with the quality and freshness. You can find them at: *www.simplynontoxiccosmetics.com*.

I believe our bodies are able to deal with some chemicals, and this is why we have a detox system which includes the liver and kidneys. But I have to wonder if our bodies were meant to deal with the onslaught of chemicals currently in our environment, our homes, our personal products, and our food. It seems we are overwhelmed. This is why it is so important to make sure your detox system is working efficiently and flushing regularly as it was designed to do.

Genetically Modified Organisms (GMO-GM Food)

Corporate agricultural companies can put their products on the market, in stores, and on your kitchen table without completing the types of long term studies that would assure the products do no harm. Most Americans do not realize GMO seeds may contaminate the DNA of seeds and plants, which have been on this earth since the beginning of time. Pollen is airborne and not containable. There is no turning back once things are contaminated. Is this a path we want to continue down? People are suffering from severe and delayed allergies to many different foods, is there a GMO connection? More than fifty countries have banned GMO's or have required strict labeling. The United States Forest Service just recently banned the planting of GMO's on National park land. Many states are individually trying to pass labeling laws right now. Do some research and learn why it's so important to be aware of the possible harm these products may bring. The Non GMO Project has a lot of accurate information. Their web site is *www.nongmoproject.org*.

Dr. Mercola at *www.mercola.com* has a wonderful interview with Jeffrey Smith of the Institute for Responsible Technology which talks about the tipping point that is coming. [4]

Here is a short preview, a link to the full article and interview is in the bibliography at the end of the book: *"In this interview,*

Jeffrey shares some of the history of his organization and what they've gone through over the last 15 years to get to this point, and why it's so important that we all act now."

"In [the beginning of] 1999, the biotech industry...was still anticipating that they could replace 95% of all commercial seeds with genetically engineered seeds within five years...But a single high profile GMO food safety scandal erupted in the middle of February 1999.

Dr. Arpad Pusztai...has been gagged and told that if he talked about what he knew, he would be sued. Well, by an order of parliament, his gag order was lifted and he could finally talk about how he discovered that genetically engineered foods were inherently unsafe and could create all sorts of damage – just from the process itself, irrespective of what gene you put in.

Seven hundred and fifty articles were written within a month, and within 10 weeks virtually every major food company committed to stop using GM ingredients in Europe because it had become a marketing liability.

They weren't instructed to do that by the government. They were instructed to do that by consumers at the top of the food chain."

According to an article from the highly reputable Institute For Responsible Technology, *"When the American Academy of Environmental Science (AAEM) was asked about the safety of GMO's they replied "Several animal studies indicate serious health risks associated with GM food," including infertility, immune problems, accelerated aging, faulty insulin regulation, and changes in major organs and the gastrointestinal system. The AAEM asked physicians to advise patients to avoid GM foods."* The article goes on to say, *"Before the FDA decided to allow GMO's into food without labeling, FDA scientists had repeatedly warned that GM foods can create unpredictable, hard-to-detect side effects, including allergies, toxins, new diseases, and nutritional problems. They urged long-term safety studies, but were ignored."* [5] If you would like more information on GMO's or would like a free shopping guide, check out their web site at *www.responsibletechnology.org/* Could this be one of the reasons why we are seeing so many allergies to foods that we've never seen before?

Also according the the Institute For Responsible Technology; *"In March 2001, the Center for Disease Control reported that food is responsible for twice the number of illnesses in the U.S. compared to estimates just seven years earlier. This increase roughly corresponds to the period when Americans have been eating GM food. Without follow-up tests, which neither the industry nor government are doing, we can't be absolutely sure if genetic engineering was the cause."* [6]

I became allergic to corn and soy during that time frame. I didn't understand I was dealing with a new allergy until I had to figure out why our horses were suddenly aborting foals and we were having difficulty getting mares pregnant. These were problems we had not experienced prior to this time. We took our horses off of the grains they had been eating, some of which were apparently GM. Within a short time, we no longer experienced any fertility or pregnancy problems. Were the problems due to GM's in their feed, I can't know for certain, but it sure seems to point in that direction. I then removed commercial corn from my diet and also saw positive effects. To this day I avoid GM feeds and food products. I won't feed my dogs any GM foods either. I have to wonder if GM feed has anything to do with the explosion of animals now having what we used to refer to as human diseases. I don't recall dogs and horses having diabetes or other autoimmune diseases prior to this time frame like they do now. Do you? Many veterinarians I've spoken with say it's a fairly recent phenomenon. Yet, only a few are asking why it's happening.

Unfortunately, current law protects the polluter more than it protects public health. People mistakenly think there's nothing they can do, but there is. Start saying "NO." Use your power as a consumer and vote with your dollar. Europeans did it and it worked. Stop purchasing the products with toxic chemicals and questionable ingredients; instead purchase products which are safer and non toxic. The safer products are plentiful, easy to find and reasonable in cost now. If just 10% to 15% of the population did this, we would see significant change because it would affect the profits of the manufacturers and they would take the necessary steps to make safer products which would benefit all consumers and widen their market appeal again.

Inflammation

Inflammation is becoming a big topic these days. I'm really glad to see people are finally paying attention to the inflammatory basis that appears to be connected to most chronic disease. It's become epidemic. It's estimated there are over 60 million people with allergies, 30 million asthmatics and 24 million with autoimmune diseases which include diabetes, celiac, lupus, rheumatoid arthritis, multiple sclerosis, thyroid disease, RSD, inflammatory bowel disease, Crone's disease, just to name a few. I know finding the causes of inflammation have been key to reducing pain and regaining function for me.

Most doctors are suppressing inflammation with drugs such as aspirin, NSAIDs (non steroidal anti-inflammatory), steroids and powerful immune suppressing medications which can have serious side effects. As I've asked before, where is the training to find and treat the underlying causes of inflammation in chronic disease? We have to find the source of the inflammation in the body and put out that fire. When I was treated 'conventionally' the focus was to suppress the overactive immune system and the severe pain with drugs. I did this for five very long years and got sicker and heavier. The side effects were horrible and I'm still dealing with damage from the drugs to this day. Looking back now I have an analogy for this type of treatment; it's like giving a person aspirin for pain and not looking for and removing the piece of glass puncturing their foot. We know it's common sense to remove the glass, yet when the abnormality shows up in blood pressure, chronic illness, inflammation, autoimmune disease, cancer, and weight loss the same common sense is not utilized.

In order to start cooling down the inflammation in my body, I had to do my best to try to remove what was causing the heat. I had to put out the fire by treating the fire, not the smoke! Smoke, in this situation, is like inflammation in that it is the symptom telling us there is fire. Just as inflammation is the symptom telling us there is imbalance –something wrong –in the body. When you ignore or don't pay attention to the inflammation you'll start seeing more and more inflammatory symptoms, like pain and swelling, over time. Eventually, the symptoms will be more prominent and noticeable in your life, and will require your full attention. This is the body trying to save itself!

Doctors are taught to treat the smoke, i.e.: the symptoms. Doctors I know tell me they were mostly taught to diagnose by symptoms, NOT by the underlying cause. Medicine today focuses on labeling a bunch of symptoms. Functional medicine and functional nutrition teach us to look for and treat the cause, not only the symptoms. It also teaches you to get curious and ask the all important question: Why are you sick?

Over the last 25 years I have spoken with a lot of doctors. There was only one medical doctor (MD) who was actually interested in understanding what I did to get out of the wheelchair and how I reversed autoimmune thyroid and rheumatoid arthritis. Only one! That still blows my mind. I don't get it! When I hear of people healing from disease I get so excited and I love to learn how they did it and what worked for them. Other types of doctors have wanted to know but not MD's. I still have a lot of healing to do and I'm interested in learning from others. Most medical doctors I've talked with are very quick to dismiss my case and other cases as anecdotal saying there is no merit! They're not even curious! Have they had their common sense pounded out of them from all of the sleepless nights of interning? I have to wonder what medical schools are doing to doctors that would cause them to not be curious about people who are reversing symptoms of disease.

I have many friends who are doctors and I have a lot of respect for them. Most of them went into medicine because they wanted to help people get better and are finding themselves trapped in a system that doesn't really help people with chronic illness because they don't know what they don't know, they aren't asking the right questions, and they don't know how to change it. The doctors who are changing and transforming the way they practice medicine are learning through functional and integrative medicine. They are the pioneers of today.

Stories like mine and many others should not be treated as mere anecdotes; they are so much more. They are ground breaking, paradigm changing truths happening right in front of our own eyes. What is it that makes a doctor or other persons not want to believe what they're seeing?

Telling Ourselves the Truth

We've talked about several reasons why it's easier to get sick these days. Now, let's go a little deeper and take a look around us. How did this nation become the home of so many sickly people?

Really look and pay attention. It seems everywhere I look, there's illness. Yet, most people will tell you they are pretty healthy. I had a friend, whom I love dearly, recently tell me "she's in good health except for diverticulitis, a close call with colon cancer, and being about 70 pounds overweight." She almost forgot to mention she has hypothyroidism. She continued to tell me that other than these things she's in good health. I first thought to myself, "Wow, that is what I used to say." I can understand her reasoning because I used to reason the same way. I now know it as denial. How is it she and most Americans (I used to be included in this group) see this list of challenges as good health? Health is the absence of dis-ease. Is she in good health? Or is she being challenged by dis-ease? Are most Americans in good health? It doesn't seem that way. Are we stupid or are we in total denial personally and as a country? How about other countries which are adopting the processed food model? My friend is a very smart and amazing woman. She is not stupid. She's a mirror of what's been happening with so many people over the last 50 years or so, myself included!

Here's a simple example: when I was in my 20's my blood pressure and cholesterol were both elevated and I was showing signs of hypoglycemia. Yet, if anyone had asked me I would have told them I was very healthy. I looked healthy on the outside, but, my body was sending me signals I didn't understand. A nutritionally trained functional practitioner would have picked up on those signals and searched to find out why I was having the blood sugar issues. They would also investigate into why my blood pressure and cholesterol were elevated. My general practitioner didn't have the training to understand the signals and would tell me not to worry because I was so young. It was much easier for me to not worry! So I didn't worry about it. I liked not having to deal with it and be truthful with myself. It allowed me to be in denial and I had no clue or care that my body was trying to tell me something was going on! I was ignoring my early warning system! Being truthful with ourselves about our health and how unhealthy this nation has become can be a bit overwhelming and frightening.

Therefore, the majority of people are currently choosing to be in denial until they get a major wakeup call, which is usually a diagnosis of disease. Then they are surprised and ask "Why me" and "How did this happen?" I know this personally, I was one of those people in denial and asking those questions. I was truly shocked because I had no clue I even had an early warning system! It may seem as if it just happened overnight with no warning. But is that really the truth? Can you look back and maybe realize there were some early signs which weren't noticed? Realizing and noticing this can be very empowering.

Toxic Relationships

We all have them and they can do as much or more harm than the toxins I've already written about. Toxic relationships can include imbalanced interactions with spouses, partners, friends, siblings, parents, co-workers and more. We all have value and our soul knows this. We all come here to bring our value. When we are put in a position or taught:

1. We are not worthy.
2. We have less value than others.
3. We should set our well being aside for others over a long term period.

This causes us to inherently go against our soul and create an internal wrestling match known as drama.

When we are very young children our 'software' is installed and we learn from and are programmed by our families, good or bad, based on their own life experiences. We then go on to teach people throughout our lives how to treat us, based on that programming. We need to re-write the program. Stop undervaluing yourself, observe your feelings and allow them importance. Step out of the fear which holds you in this pattern of relationships. Know you can change the dynamics of your relationships. When you do you will find an unshakeable peace no one can take from you. Find a good coach to help you through the various stages and know you are worth every penny and hour invested in the process.

There's a lot of good news here. We can learn to notice and listen to the early signals our body communicates to us. I have learned that asking a question doesn't have to be frightening or overwhelming. When I have asked the questions I've learned I can take simple steps to change things in positive ways. I now understand I have the opportunity and ability to take preventive steps and build better health. I have given myself permission and learned to say no. As a nation, if we say no, maybe we won't have to continue experiencing epidemics of chronic illness everywhere. Maybe we can have an epidemic of wellness!

Would you like to be able to take simple steps to help you create and bring better health to your life? What I needed to create better health was some hope, support, and a little guidance in the right direction. I also had to find my courage. I had to gather courage to be able to let go of habits and dependencies I had been taught, to be able to say no, and to be able to explore what my true potential was. I have been doing it by taking baby steps, consistent baby steps; one day, one week, one month, one year at a time.

I believe it's time to be honest with ourselves and admit what's not working and what needs to be changed. It's time for a 180 Degree Wellness Revolution. We have to turn this (healthcare crisis) ship around before it crashes into the jagged rocks that lie ahead. Are you ready to join me?

In the following chapters, I'm going to help you learn about recognizing opportunities for healing. These are steps which have helped me personally, and many others, to build health and feel better. I'm not saying this will cure you and I'm not telling you what to do. Nobody can tell you what to do unless you allow it. Your health is your responsibility and only you can make decisions regarding what is best for you and your body. I don't know if I'll be able to fully answer your questions, but please know it's okay if you disagree with something I say. I'm not trying to convince you to do or believe anything. I simply hope to raise your curiosity and your awareness.

We must wake up from our sleepy denial and see just how unhealthy we've become, what is behind the choices to allow poor health and then make some real actionable changes. It's all about educating ourselves and removing the denial. It's about being willing to see and value feedback which asks us to stretch our beliefs and our comfort zones. Our doctors have not been educated to heal, they've been educated to prescribe for symptoms and create a retirement fund for pharmaceutical companies and their executives. Much of our food is not real anymore. Poisons are applied to what could be real food. We are allowing this! It doesn't have to be this way.

What I would like to show you is a path you don't have to walk alone. We are all unique individuals and what works for one person may not work for another. Choosing to follow some of the basic steps and finding what works for you, can create opportunities for healing. Your quality of life and well-being can increase as a result.

4
FOOD AS MEDICINE

Some of the most powerful medicines
can be found growing in a yard.

Food is our fuel. We cannot remain healthy and function optimally when we dilute the quality of our food/fuel. Remember the car analogy... If you add sugar or soda to your car's fuel how would it run? Is a car designed to perform with this type of additive in its fuel? Could soda or sugar damage the internal mechanisms of your car's motor? Would your car function optimally if water or another fluid was added to the oil? The answer to all of these questions is no. Your car would spit and sputter as you try to start it and the motor may never run again, leaving you with a high repair bill. We recognize we don't want to put the wrong fuel in our cars because the damage could cost us greatly. We don't seem to acknowledge our bodies can be similar in certain ways to that of a car. Look at the many additives in food which didn't exist a few decades ago. How are they affecting us? Unfortunately, we have not been well informed of the consequences that may happen when chemical additives are placed in food or water. We are not readily warned of possible negative affects to our internal systems and organs.

Why should you learn to read labels and be concerned with ingredients in your food? Simply put, food can be medicine or a poison. It gives us health and energy or takes health and energy away. Once you realize the effect of the food you eat, understanding food ingredients becomes essential. I'm not saying we can possibly avoid all chemicals and toxins; reducing exposure is going to be imperative for our future health and the health of our children. There is a big difference between conventional/ chemical and organically grown foods. I have found awareness of this fact is crucial if you want to remain healthy and especially if you are trying to regain health after illness.

Food today is very different from the food of 60+ years ago. Plants have been hybridized and bred for certain characteristics without thought as to possible side effects as a result. A good example of this is wheat. Wheat has been bred to have higher gluten content. This is because gluten helps bread rise and makes it fluffier. Wheat, which used to stand five feet tall, is now bred to be a few feet tall making it easier to harvest. We don't think much about making changes and breeding certain characteristics into a crop. We only imagine it will create an easier to work with commercial product. We are now beginning to realize the big experiment playing out in our health. The gluten protein has been modified to the extent our bodies may perceive it as a foreign invader! Some people are more affected than others, kind of like the canaries in the coal mine. Gluten intolerance is showing up everywhere and in all ages.

Farmers are being taught they must use chemicals to grow food. They are even taught this in college! There is a war mentality in the field and they think they have to kill everything. The thought process might go kind of like this; see weed – pick poison – kill weed. So, they spray their crops with chemicals that are neurotoxic and somehow think the neurotoxicity magically disappears when they harvest the crop and before it ends up on your table.

An article published on *www.naturalnews.com* titled "Organic food contains up to 60% more antioxidants: study", refers to "the largest review of published data on organic food ever conducted. An international team of researchers from Newcastle University in the UK looked at 343 peer-reviewed studies comparing organic and conventional crops, and came to the conclusion that organic produce is higher in antioxidants, lower in toxic heavy metals and much less contaminated with pesticide and herbicide residues. They determined that, overall, organic produce contains between 18 and 69% higher polyphenolic content compared to conventional produce, which is substantial considering the amazing health benefits of this class of antioxidants. Polyphenols, as you may already know, have been linked to a reduced risk of chronic disease, including serious cardiovascular and neurodegenerative diseases, as well as cancer." [7] This study, "Organic vs Non-Organic Food", was published in the *British Journal of Nutrition* on July 11, 2014. [8]

In an article published in the *Rodale News* titled "The Truth About Organic" the author was referring to "The Farming Systems Trial" at *Rodale Institute* and states, "...researchers did conclude that organic food contained significantly lower levels of pesticide residues, something previous research suggests could help protect kids from autism and ADHD, among other ills. United States Department of Agriculture testing routinely finds pesticide residues considered unsafe for children on conventionally grown – not organic – produce samples, including apples, peaches, plums, pears, grapes, blueberries, strawberries, and raisons." The article went on to say, "Eating organic coincides with a massive drop in disease-causing pesticides in your body. The enormous benefit of eating organic produce is that it reduces pesticide exposure by 90%. This has been proven in studies conducted at Harvard, the University of Washington, and the Centers for Disease Control and Prevention," explains pediatrician Phil Landrigan, MD, professor and chair of Preventive Medicine at Mount Sinai School of Medicine in New York City. "Reduction of exposure to pesticides reduces risk of neurological injury and certain cancers. I advise my patients to choose organic whenever possible." [9]

Are you beginning to see why paying attention to ingredients in food helped me get out of a wheelchair? Well-grown food not only tastes better, it promotes building of health. The "Farming Systems Trial" at *Rodale Institute* is the longest running, side by side comparison of organic and chemical agriculture. The study began in 1981 and has clearly demonstrated organic farming is better equipped to feed us now and into the future, lower greenhouse gases and promote a cleaner, less polluted environment.[10] In my opinion farming programs need to move away from synthetic chemicals and fertilizers and focus on implementation of organic practices that do not poison.

Organically grown produce does not necessarily have to be certified organic. It might be, but it doesn't have to be. Many small farms cannot afford the cost nor have the resources to keep up the paperwork involved in being certified organic, though the farm may follow or even exceed organic rules. Nutritional content can vary. Just because food is certified organic doesn't mean it is more nutritious than the food your local farmer is growing organically. Nutritionally rich food is a result of good soil building practices which support and feed biology in the soil. Conventional farming practices use synthetic fertilizer and chemicals, which can kill biology in the soil. When you support local growers who utilize good soil and nutrient building practices by purchasing from them, you are supporting your own health and the health of the community. You'll be amazed at how delicious well-grown food is. You really can taste the difference.

Reasons I value organic food:

- Organic food doesn't contain synthetic pesticides, endocrine disruptors, GM (Genetically Modified) crops and GM ingredients.
- Organic animals are prohibited from using antibiotics, growth hormones, and genetically modified vaccines.
- Organic animals aren't fed arsenic, animal remains or slaughterhouse waste, reducing the risks of CJD; the human version of mad cow disease.
- Organic foods aren't fertilized with toxic sewage sludge or coal waste, or irrigated with E. coli contaminated sewage water.
- Organic food is not irradiated. Cats fed a diet of irradiated food got multiple sclerosis within 3-4 months.[11] [12]

This is just a small sample of the information you will find at *www.organicconsumers.org* if you're looking for more information. The Organic Consumers Association web site is a wonderful resource on certified organic food.

Keeping a Budget

Organic food can sometimes be more expensive than non-organic food. Have you ever wondered why? The organic price is typically reflective of the true cost of growing real food. Subsidies make the unhealthy foods appear cheaper than healthy foods at the cash register. Why? One reason is because less than 10% of

USDA subsidies are spent on healthy foods like vegetables and fruits. Instead subsidies are paid to megafarms for the mass production of GM corn and GM soy, along with a few other grains, which are being used as cheap ingredients in feeds and processed foods. Small organic farms growing healthier foods are not usually subsidized by taxpayer monies as many of the megafarms are.

In 2012, the most recent available data, agricultural subsidies in the United States amounted to just over 30 billion dollars! This is your tax dollars! Which food is really more expensive? If you factor in taxes collected to pay subsidies to farms using synthetic chemicals, the cost of conventional – chemically grown food goes up dramatically. Corporate megafarms are being paid really well to produce food which may be poisoned and lower in nutrition. Not only do we citizens pay in subsidies, we also pay in healthcare costs. Getting sick is not cheap. So, I ask again...which food is really more expensive?

I have a budget and I'm sure many of you do too. I have found it expensive to NOT eat organically. How much does it cost to go to a doctor or hospital because you're sick? How expensive is chronic illness, autoimmune disease or cancer? I know medical expenses have been terribly high for me. Pay the farmer now or pay the doctor and hospital later. I personally prefer to pay the farmer. When I stopped shopping for sodas and processed refined foods I saw a significant savings. I simply allocated that money to foods that would build health and help me feel better. I also grow much of my own food and this lowers my grocery bill substantially.

Here are a few suggestions to find reasonably priced organically grown foods:

- Buy a CSA share (Commmunity Supported Agriculture). Check web sites such as *LocalHarvest.org* to find a CSA near you.

- Buy 'in season'. Peak season brings much lower prices, preserve food by freezing or canning. Buy it now and freeze it for later!
- Go to the local Farmers Market, food will be cheaper and fresher. Ask about their farming methods. Ask about bulk discounts if you'll be preserving large amounts of food.
- Join a food co-op. Check web sites such as *www.cooperativegrocer.coop* and *LocalHarvest.org* to find a co-op near you.
- Join a buying club. You may be able to get 30% to 40% off retail price for organic food and products. Buying clubs are able to order direct from the distributor.
- Grow your own. Start small and simple. Lettuce, carrots, beets and radishes are easy. Keep it simple and add more produce as you gain confidence.

Is the cost of organically grown food really higher and conventional/chemically grown food really less expensive? Synthetic chemical use in agriculture has risen greatly over the years, coinciding with nutrition levels in food going down. All the while, health care costs have gone up significantly. The cost of disease care is bankrupting this country, yet we still think 'cheap food' is less expensive. Is it? The truth is, these questions are not being asked.

Conventional?

Why are chemical agriculture and chemical (patented drugs) medicine labeled as conventional agriculture and conventional medicine? Conventional implies normal, standard or traditional. In the dictionary conventional is defined as "usual or established;

using well-established methods or styles." Most chemicals used in farming today didn't exist before World War I. The chemicals were manufactured for chemical warfare. Now they are applied to your food. War is created in the fields against insects and weeds. How can such chemicals be considered normal, standard or traditional in farming? The normal, traditional, well established way to grow food, the way food has been grown for thousands of years is now more like organic. We pay a premium to have cleaner food, grown the way it was always grown before chemical use began. Isn't it a bit strange that we've been led to believe a chemical warfare type of agriculture is the well established or best method when the chemicals have only existed for a very short time period in history? Why aren't farmers concerned about the exposure to neurotoxins they and their family are receiving by living on the farm and by eating this food?

I've been growing food organically for over 25 years. Time in the garden is relaxing and therapeutic for me. If you've never done it give it a try! It's fun eating food you have grown with your own two hands. As a Master Gardener, I get many questions about insects and plant disease when volunteering at my local agriculture extension office. They are probably two of the biggest frustrations gardeners have. I'll tell you what I tell them. Insects are not attracted to well grown, nutrient rich foods. Insects are God's garbage crew and they will eat food which is poor in condition. Plant disease mostly affects unhealthy plants that are not receiving a proper balance of nutrients. (I will go into this concept further in chapter 9, explaining where nutrition comes from.)

Transitioning to a healthier lifestyle can be a challenge and at first may seem overwhelming. From what I've observed, making smaller gradual changes leads to more success and is easier. Start by learning to read labels and PLU codes on produce. PLU code basics:

- Conventional produce; vegetables and fruit have a 4 digit number usually beginning with 3 or 4.
- Organic certified; will have 5 digit numbers and begin with 9. Example code: Banana 94011
- Genetically Modified (GM); vegetables and fruit begin with 8. Example code: Banana 84011

Add nutritious organically grown food into your diet, especially fresh fruits and vegetables. Get familiar with the "Dirty Dozen", foods with the highest pesticide concentrations. You can find this information at the web site *www.ewg.org* or search it. Allocate time into your schedule for cooking, make it a fun family event. Don't focus on what you have to remove. Focus on the new foods you get to explore! By adding more and more foods you will be 'crowding out' the unhealthy foods and replacing them gradually with foods better for you. This method of crowding out is taught at the Institute for Integrative Nutrition® (IIN®) and is very helpful. I suggest eating foods your great grandparents ate, utilizing as much organically grown produce as possible to avoid harmful pesticides and chemicals.

5
THE PATH TO BETTER HEALTH

When a child learns to walk, they crawl and then stand. When first standing up they wobble and fall over. They get up again, take a step, and oops...fall again. They keep getting up. A child doesn't believe falling down means they have failed. They just keep trying until they get it right. They don't give up. They stand, then they walk on.

You must first try to understand why there is malfunction to improve health and prevent illness. You want to be aware of patterns that can contribute to dysfunction and avoid them. Without understanding you are bound to continue repeating the patterns that helped you arrive where you are today. To improve function you must look to see where there are imbalances. You have to become a detective and search for an underlying cause. Getting really honest about your personal habits, good and bad is important. Learning to judge less and appreciate yourself more is helpful.

I always suggest to people to begin by looking at the food you eat, the water you drink, the way you chew and digest your food, along with the personal products you use. You can start making simple changes in your habits and in your kitchen while you are preparing to put your support team in place. If you have no clue how to begin looking at food, there is a 10 day cleanse available on my web site; *www.cultivatinghealth.org*. This cleanse can help guide you through the process, give you recipes to follow, and teach you about food that can heal and food that can harm along with addressing stressors. It is an option if you need help. If you are eating processed foods, be aware they could be leaching nutrients from your body.

If you need help understanding what is toxic and what is not, I suggest purchasing the book *The Pure Cure* written by naturopath Sharyn Wynters in partnership with founder and former publisher of *Alternative Medicine* magazine Burton Goldberg, LHD. This book will always have a place on my bookshelf. It is the best reference book on toxins and solutions I have found. The research is thorough, easy to comprehend and obviously comes from many years of deep understanding. It is available on Amazon.com.

I was diagnosed with autoimmune hypothyroid disease over 20 years ago. I had the typical symptoms of puffiness around my face, poor eyebrow growth on the outer third of my eyebrows, weight gain, fatigue, thinning hair and extremely dry skin. My doctor was knowledgeable about thyroid testing and knew to run a complete thyroid panel, not just the medical standard TSH and T4. The blood test results showed I had low thyroid function and I was producing auto-antibodies, which indicated autoimmune dysfunction. He prescribed Synthroid and I took it for over 10 years. It helped some, but it didn't help a lot. I took Synthroid until I figured a way to reverse the autoimmunity and heal my thyroid. It took quite a few years, a lot of research and patience to peel the onion that was me, but I have found success in this functional holistic approach. I kept asking two questions: what was the malfunction causing my thyroid to be underactive and why would my body create auto-antibodies to destroy its own thyroid? I had to figure out where healing opportunities were and what I could do to turn it around. The answers came in bits and pieces over the years with gut healing, adrenal healing and nutrition being a huge part. I didn't want to be dependent on taking a synthetic drug like Synthroid for the rest of my life. I also didn't want to have to replace the synthetic drug with natural products that I would have to take for the rest of my life. My goal was to restore complete function if at all possible.

Chances are, the food you are eating is greatly lacking in nutrition. Especially if you are eating fast food or processed food in a box. I'm sure you've heard the saying, "You are what you eat." My experience has shown me that is not totally accurate, it should be "You are what you absorb." If you are not absorbing appropriate levels of nutrients, you are effectively in a state of malnutrition. There are a great number of people who eat three meals a day and are starving for nourishment. You must get nutrients into the body and it's crucial they are able to be absorbed and utilized. The gut lining can also become inflamed and permeable, allowing undigested food molecules to pass into the blood. This damage to the intestinal lining is called Leaky Gut and I'll explain more in a few pages. Years ago I had learned of this concept and understood that healing my gut was critical for healing the rest of my body. My gut was so damaged at that time I was not able to absorb nutrients even though I was eating really nutritious foods! No wonder I felt hungry and craved sweets all the time! I had to prioritize healing my gut.

Autoimmunity

What is autoimmunity and how does it occur? It is one example of the body malfunctioning. Your immune system is your defense system against invaders. Much of your immune system is in your gut, approximately 80% according to scientists. The immune system has its own internal army whose job is to determine friend from foe. It has to know what is 'you' and what is 'other'. When your immune system gets confused and targets its own tissues, autoimmunity occurs. Then, your body redirects its attack on the thyroid, gut, skin, joints, brain or sometimes the whole body.

As mentioned earlier, many conventional treatments can make you feel worse and create additional inflammation. That is what happened to me. I had no idea or real understanding of the ingredients and the side effects of the treatments and how they could damage my body. Taking anti-inflammatory drugs can possibly lead to intestinal damage, kidney damage, depression, osteoporosis, muscle loss, diabetes, infections or more. It is possible that some anti-inflammatory drugs may be helpful when used as a short term solution to provide symptom relief while the root cause of pain or disease is aggressively pursued. In my situation they were being used as the only treatment, a long term solution, and they failed miserably. They caused harm. This needs to change.

What did I do to reverse autoimmune diseases wreaking havoc within me? I had to first stop adding to the stress my body was already dealing with. I had to question everything! To start, I kept it simple. Reducing easily identifiable stressors such as toxins in food and drinks was very important. **I ate with the understanding that any food going into my mouth was either giving nutrients to my body or stealing nutrients from it.**

First action steps you can take:

1. Look in your pantry and determine which foods are the worst. Mark those for removal or replacement. I went

through my pantry and removed the worst of the chemical and non-nutritive foods. Not easy since we were financially stressed. Each week I would replace one or two foods I knew had chemicals in them with foods which didn't have chemicals. I soon had a nice supply of clean foods.
2. Eliminate sodas. When I stopped drinking sodas I saved a lot of money!
3. Drink plenty of clean filtered well or spring water.
4. Talk with your functional or integrative doctor and follow his/her advice on modifying medications. I removed many and consistently continued to wean off of prescription synthetic medications.
5. Remove cooking pans and utensils coated with chemicals, replace them gradually with non toxic cookware and utensils.
6. Grow your own food or buy and support a local farm! I started once again growing a lot of my own food. What I didn't grow, I aimed to purchase from a local farmer/gardener I knew. This cut my grocery bill by 70%.

These steps helped me to lessen the inflammatory process, which had taken over my body. This was the very beginning of creating wellness in a not very well body. They are relatively easy steps under most circumstances. It was a bit challenging from a wheelchair, but my amazing friend Jyl helped me with some of it and I am forever grateful to her. I would love to have been able to get rid of all the toxic things in my kitchen in one sweep, but this illness created a financial crisis. I did the best I could with what resources were available. I found that when I began using non toxic products, I no longer wanted to use the toxic stuff. It was so easy to let them go at that point. It really didn't take long to get rid of the products that weren't good for me and my kitchen was less crowded.

I remember feeling very uneasy about being criticized and made to come across as irresponsible and careless because my choices were what most would call "unconventional". My only options were to continue taking the anti-inflammatory and many other medications I had been prescribed for the rest of my life or to change my path. I knew I had to change my path even though most people around me disagreed. I needed to get to the root cause and stop masking symptoms. It was an incredibly lonely decision, there wasn't much support available in the mid 1990's for this type of lifestyle change. I became my own 'food as medicine' experiment to see if I could really get better without the use of a dozen or more prescribed drugs.

After a few weeks of being off of some of the medications I noticed I was more alert and had better comprehension, so I began studying medical and nutritional journals. I also studied herbs and Chinese/Eastern medical philosophy. My memory was still horrendous so I took plenty of notes. After approximately six months I was really seeing some benefits. I was beginning to get a tiny bit of feeling back in my left foot. I wasn't sure I'd ever have use of my left leg again. To me, this was monumental and I was so excited! I delved into even more research and more alternative medical journals. The Internet wasn't yet available, so I did it using basic research methods and taking lots of notes when I could on my "good days".

I began learning about the immune system and the gut connection, oxidative stress, nutrition, the endocrine system, plant and soil nutrition, toxic dental work and heavy metal toxicity. I say 'began' because twenty years later I am still learning and research is more and more available. As I mentioned previously, in my own healing the gut has been central to strengthening my immune system and creating an environment where inflammation would be triggered less often. Science is just beginning to discover the fundamental importance of food quality. The food you eat directly determines and affects the type of and levels of certain bacteria in your gut. Changing the diet and therefore the environment of the gut will change the bacteria, which will thrive. This will be explained more in chapter 6, *The Power of Digestion.*

I realized there wasn't a quick fix, especially since insurance doesn't pay for this type of care and it would have to come out of my pocket. I would have to save money and do it step by step as I could financially afford it. I also realized I would need to heal my gut before I could consider removing any toxic dental work or heavy metals like mercury, due to the possibility of reabsorbing the toxins through a leaky, permeable gut.

Changing my diet and making lifestyle adjustments to reduce stressors were very important steps and are crucial to healing. In addition, I began working with a Naturopath, an Oriental Doctor (OMD) and a Chiropractor to figure out where the problems were coming from. Here are a few things I concentrated on, not necessarily in the order in which I did them:

1. Learned which foods fuel me and which foods slow me down
2. Took serious steps to reduce stress in my life
3. Used easily digestible nutritional support
4. Tested for hidden and delayed food allergies via elimination diet and labs
5. Gut Healing
6. Heavy metal toxicity testing
7. Celiac and Gluten sensitivity testing
8. Checked for hidden infections
9. Exercise as tolerated

10. Dental amalgams were eventually removed by a qualified holistic dentist using the proper protocols

I often get asked what was the one most important thing I did to start getting better. There's never just one thing that has gone wrong when a person becomes ill, especially if the illness is prolonged. The body has many systems and they all work harmoniously together to keep it well. It all functions together as one. **One of the most important overall things I did was to reduce toxins that I put in my body.** You can reduce toxins by educating yourself about the foods you are eating and the drugs you are taking. Replace toxic or allergenic items with items that are not. It made a huge difference in my life and set me up for future success.

Another critical step to healing you will hear me say over and over again is gut health. **Your gut is not just your waistline or your belly – it is the doorway to health for your immune system and your brain.** The immune system and gut are intimately linked. Close to 80% of your immune system is located in your gut. The digestive system can be the first point of exposure to pathogens (the bad bacteria and viruses) and for this reason it needs to be healthy. I learned through experience that when gut healing begins symptoms start disappearing. Isn't that cool? Gut mucosa connects with immune cells within the body. T-cells and B-cells defend the inside of your digestive tract. There are also strains of friendly gut flora (microbes) living inside the intestines which are essential for keeping the immune system healthy and thriving. The gut microbes are an ally to the immune cells and enhance their ability to defend the intestinal walls preventing invaders and infections from passing through. Without this help the immune system will be overwhelmed and less efficient.

Leaky Gut

What causes Leaky Gut? According to Amy Myers, MD, a renowned leader in Functional medicine, the main sources are toxins, foods or infections. Toxins may include medications like non steroidal anti-inflammatory drugs (NSAIDs), steroids, acid-reducing drugs, antibiotics and environmental toxins like mercury, lead, BPA from plastics and pesticides. Gluten is suspected to be the main inflammatory food, though in some people dairy, sugar or alcohols are inflammatory and suspected to contribute as well. The most common infectious causes are Candida overgrowth, small intestinal bacteria overgrowth (SIBO) and intestinal parasites. [13]

The gut is designed to be permeable to allow very small molecules through its protective lining in order for us to absorb vital nutrients. This is how food becomes nutrition once it's properly broken down and digested. The gut lining protects you from absorbing things that are or could become toxic to you. One of the basic functions of the cells lining the intestinal wall is to regulate this permeability and allow in only the molecules which are supposed to pass through. What happens with Leaky Gut is kind of equivalent to someone taking a pair of scissors and poking larger holes in the gut lining. These holes can allow larger molecules, undigested food particles, microbes and more to escape the intestines and enter the bloodstream, where they're not supposed to be. Once in the bloodstream they can travel throughout your body. Your immune system doesn't like having these molecules in there and it reacts by marking them as foreign invaders and attacking them just as it would a pathogen. This can result in a war inside your body. The attack can happen in tissues in different parts of your body or in the intestinal track. Your immune system may begin assaulting its own healthy joints and tissues. Then, your body may now see corn, bread or other foods as an enemy. The question to ask is – why is your gut permeable? What is cutting holes and in what part of your body is the war taking place? For someone diagnosed with Celiac disease, it might show up in the intestine. When they eat bread products with gluten, the gluten starts traveling through their body and due to their genetic predisposition, the body wages war on the small intestine, destroying the healthy gut tissue and possibly more. For someone with Hashimoto's thyroiditis the body wages war on the thyroid, targeting healthy thyroid tissue and possibly more.

Here are some (not all) of the potential signs of Leaky Gut:

- Digestive issues such as gas, bloating, diarrhea, constipation, irritable bowel syndrome (IBS), inflammatory bowel disease (IBD)
- Seasonal allergies or asthma
- Food allergies or intolerances
- Diagnosis of Candida overgrowth
- Diagnosis of chronic fatigue, fibromyalgia or autoimmune diseases such as lupus, rheumatoid arthritis, psoriasis, Hashimoto's thyroiditis, Graves, MS, Type 1 diabetes, or celiac disease
- Hormonal imbalances like PMS or PCOS
- Depression, anxiety, chronic headaches, brain fog, ADD or ADHD
- Skin issues such as acne, eczema or rosacea

What can you do to heal Leaky Gut? If you suspect you are dealing with a permeable gut, I recommend you research this subject deeper and work with a Functional or Integrative practitioner experienced and successful in gut healing for the quickest and best results. You will likely need to have some testing done, which I will go into in a later chapter.

I will briefly highlight a few things for you. These are things I have learned and you will need to pay attention to if healing a leaky gut. First, it is imperative to remove the toxic or inflammatory foods for a certain period of time. You can do this with an elimination diet or through testing. If there are intestinal infections you need to have them treated and removed. Support digestive function so food molecules are completely broken down and digested. That support may consist of digestive enzymes, hydrochloric acid betaine and bile acids. You will need to restore a healthy balance of good bacteria in your gut. This can be done with commercial probiotics, fermented or cultured foods like kefir, yogurt, sauerkraut, miso or Kimchi. I prefer water/coconut water kefir and sauerkraut. Be aware that people dealing with intestinal infections such as SIBO may sometimes be unable to utilize fermented or cultured foods until the infection is cleared and healing has begun. To repair the gut you must provide good nutrition. I've also used L-glutamine, an amino acid which is known for helping rejuvenate the gut lining along with a short period of colostrum. Don't forget that to heal the body, you must heal the gut.

Cancer

I have to wonder if cancer, in many cases, is a result of malnutrition, toxins, and a leaky gut. The lack of nutrition or deficiency of certain important nutrients combined with exposure to certain toxic elements can surely affect us at the cellular level, causing the suppression of **apoptosis**. Apoptosis is programmed cell death. If a cell is damaged, our body knows to get rid of it before it becomes a cancerous cell out of control. This is a natural survival mechanism. Apoptosis, a protective mechanism of programmed cell suicide where one cell will kill itself to protect the rest of the cells in the body, is not working if cancer is present.

A cancer cell is **not** a normal cell. It is a cell that has morphed and the immune system is unable to control it. The cancer cell will use its own survival mechanism, which is to throw out seed like a dying plant or tree does at the end of summer to ensure its longevity. It wants to replicate itself for survival. The cancer cell must have a supportive environment it can survive in. This environment would lack nutrients while containing a sugar/fuel source. Cancer thrives in a faulty immune system, one which is not functioning properly.

Dr. Buttar, a highly respected osteopath doctor who specializes in detoxing and treating cancer patients stated in a recent interview on the Robert Scott Bell radio show, "Cancer, remember is by definition impossible if you have an intact immune system. If your immune system is functional and working well there is no way you can get cancer, that's just the bottom line... If you didn't have an issue with your immune system, you wouldn't have cancer." [14]

They go on in this interview to talk about how they've met people who are diagnosed with cancer who don't understand how they could suddenly get sick because they've not been sick in 20 years. People automatically equate never getting colds or fevers with being healthy. What those people may not have realized is not getting sick could actually be an indicator their immune system isn't functioning well. Not always, but it is a possibility which shouldn't be overlooked. If you think you are healthy because you haven't been sick a day in your life you could be wrong. It's not normal to not ever be sick. The immune system is designed to respond to any type of imbalance or challenge and should give an appropriate response such as a runny nose, sneezing, fever or sore throat. Not a chronic response, but a response to a virus or acute disease. When you get a fever or runny nose, it means your immune system is working! Of course you should be able to get over it quickly when the immune system is working well. If you never get a runny nose or fever you may have a false sense of security. There may be a few individuals that could have a super strong immune system and simply never get sick; and they certainly do exist. However, the common misconception is if you never get sick you're healthy. Many times I've had friends say after being diagnosed with a serious illness or cancer, that it was a complete surprise to them, because they were one of those people who "never got sick". When your body responds by becoming reactive – symptomatic, fever, etc. – this is a good sign. Understand what the response means and ask yourself if you want to suppress a normal reaction before reaching for a pill that could tell your immune system to stop doing its job.

In a healthy body with a functioning immune system, a truly healthy cell that became damaged would destroy itself and the immune system would remove it. We really need to ask what was missing or off balance which would allow a healthy cell to change into a cancerous cell? Nutrients? Was there a toxic exposure or burden? A combination of both; a deficiency and toxicity is likely. What was the trigger?

Our bodies have more industrial pollutants and toxins to deal with while at the same time there are more deficits in the nutritional value of our food than ever. Soils are depleted and in poor shape with nutrients being locked up and unavailable. Neurotoxic pesticides are sprayed on the soils and foods. This has an accumulative effect on our cells.

Ty Bolinger recently created a wonderful video series called: "The Truth About Cancer; The Quest for the Cures." In this series he interviews 29 doctors, experts, and survivors who educate and show you exactly how to prevent and treat cancer. It's a must see and can be found at *www.thetruthaboutcancer.com*.

My steps to healing began 20 years ago. Why has it taken so long? Because we have a broken healthcare system which makes it difficult to get supportive, affordable, functional care that builds health and wellness. I also suffered setbacks, some things were not addressed completely, and other injuries complicated the situation. It's a shame insurance fails to support and provide the care which could have made setbacks less challenging, less expensive and easier to recuperate from. Functional holistic based care could benefit everyone with better health and lower healthcare costs by alleviating many major illnesses and surgeries through prevention. One of the things not fully addressed for me was the proper functioning of my adrenals and hormones. (Adrenals and hormones must be healthy and functioning.) Doctors thought they were addressing them, but as usual it was mostly symptom relief without really looking for the cause.

On the positive side, this is dramatically changing. Scientist and researchers are beginning to acknowledge that there is a connection between the gut, adrenals, liver, immune system and more, something many cultures and societies have known and honored since long ago. The subjects of the micro-biome and epigenetics are finally beginning to get some of the attention deserved. They are two very important subjects you will be hearing a lot about in the near future and I'm pleased to see this happening.

After 20 years I am doing much better. I am still in recovery mode and working to heal the deep damage. I sometimes wonder if I may have been able to recover in just a few years and suffered much less damage had the functional integrative care I am familiar with today been available to me years ago. This is why I have written this book and want to bring awareness to what I have experienced and learned to you and others.

Functional nutrition and healthcare has made such a difference in my life that after completing training at the Institute for Integrative Nutrition in New Your City, I went on to train as a **Functional Diagnostic Nutrition® practitioner (FDN)**. I found the missing piece!

A Functional Diagnostic Nutritionist is trained to look for the cause of malfunction. Some people refer to the FDN as a health detective. FDN's do not practice medicine and do not diagnose. We look for the root cause and find opportunities for healing. I am now addressing the missing pieces and resetting hormonal pathways. It will be a great day when everyone understands the hormone connections and every doctor has an FDN and a holistically trained Health Coach on his or her team.

6
STRESS

"Remembering that I'll be dead soon is the most important tool I've ever encountered to help me make the big choices in life. Because almost everything – all external expectations, all pride, all fear of embarrassment or failure – these things just fall away in the face of death, leaving only what is truly important." -Steve Jobs

We are all stressed. The world we live in rewards and encourages stress in a big way. We are so used to daily stress we think of it as normal. It seems inevitable in our lives so we just accept it right? Well, maybe we shouldn't accept it. Perhaps we need to change this way of thinking. **Stress is wreaking havoc on our wellness, our minds, and our bodies.** A certain level of stress is indeed present at times in our lives, but the level of stress most people deal with today should not be what we consider normal.

Let's have a basic lesson in stress physiology. The part of the brain which controls what we don't have to consciously think about like breathing, digestion, heart beating, etc., has two modes. The sympathetic mode is the "stress" fight or flight mode. The parasympathetic mode is the relaxation mode. There is no in between area. You are in one or the other. If you're not in a relaxed parasympathetic mode you're in a stressed sympathetic mode. It is that simple.

Basically, if you are in a sympathetic stress mode, your body is preparing for fight or flight. It thinks it's fighting for survival. Biochemical changes occur in your body to help prepare for fight or flight.

Stress can:

- Compromise digestion. You could be eating the most nutritious diet out there, but if you're stressed out your body won't be able to digest and absorb well. Stress slows the digestive system down significantly because it needs to direct the body's energy to survival. This can cause digestive distress, poor nutrient absorption which in turn can promote things like nutrient deficiencies, poor immune function and decreased gut flora.
- Create hormone imbalance. The body in sympathetic mode will prioritize the production of stress hormones such as cortisol, a fat storing hormone. Other hormones will be under produced and steroid metabolic pathways can be disturbed.
- Increase blood pressure, triglycerides, cholesterol LDL and heart rate.
- Increase inflammation and oxidation, speeding up the aging process.
- Stress can also affect the skin causing rashes, acne or other reactions. It can worsen conditions such as psoriasis, rosacea and eczema. This is oftentimes a

subtle indication of what is going on in the body, another signal.

I could go on and on about the affects negative stress has on your body. The main thing I want you to understand is your body doesn't know the difference between stressing over a deadline or escaping and running from a bear that is chasing you in the woods. The response the body mounts is the same for either. What would it be like if you had to run from a bear in the woods daily? What toll would that kind of stress have on your body?

Long term stress exposure can lead to significant health problems. It's not something to take lightly. Chronic stress disturbs just about every system in your body. Some of the health problems that can be caused or exacerbated by stress are: Pain, heart disease, sleep disorders, depression, weight problems, and autoimmune disease. This is what chronic stress could be doing to you!

Steps to create your own sympathetic stress relief program at home:

1. Become aware of when you are in sympathetic stress mode. Breathe and relax.
2. Look at your daily life and be very honest with yourself about what is causing you great stress. What can you take out of your life or say no to that would reduce your level of stress? It may not be your highest stressor, but something which is there day to day.
3. Think of something you could do daily that really relaxes and nurtures you. It might be a nice afternoon walk, prayer/meditation or a 20 minute power nap. Maybe it's dancing to fun music for 10 minutes! Whatever it may be, commit to adding this one thing into your daily routine.

4. Each week look at your stressors and continue to remove the ones you can. Learn to say no when you need to. Find a balance which allows you to enjoy life while staying predominantly in parasympathetic mode.

7
THE POWER OF DIGESTION

You are what you absorb!

I've heard it said many times that up to 90% of degenerative disease is due to weak digestion along with poor assimilation and absorption of foods. We have an interesting situation today because it's much more difficult to get nutrient rich foods than in the past, even though there is more food and food-resembling substances available on the market. It's important to choose real foods that give us nutrients.

The way food is grown makes a huge difference in its nutrient profile. On the other hand, you must be able to properly absorb and utilize the nutrients available. The best food in the world will not help us if we are unable to digest and absorb what we eat. You are what you absorb AND eliminate. If we are unable to eliminate efficiently our bodies turn into toxic sewers, which is the perfect environment for diseases like cancer and autoimmune conditions. **The ability to absorb nutrients and remove waste is critical to your body's ability to function.** Many things can affect your digestive power. Let's take a look at some of them beginning with stress.

Stress and Digestion

Managing stress is essential to maintaining or restoring healthy digestive function. Have you ever had an upset stomach or felt nauseous when things are stressful or had a 'nervous stomach' prior to an exam? Most of us are used to eating as quickly as possible due to time restraints. Many people eat while sitting at a desk or while on the go running errands. We're given very short periods of time to eat even as young children in school. Many European countries are quite the opposite and for good reason. We unfortunately live most of the time in sympathetic mode, unaware we should be giving concern to proper digestion of our food. When eating, it's best to remain in a relaxed state for awhile. In the previous chapter I explained basic stress physiology and how the sympathetic (SNS) and the parasympathetic (PSNS) nervous systems function. It is really important to understand how this system is designed and affects your health.

Digestion stops when you are stressed or grieving. Try not to eat when upset, dealing with a stressful situation, or exercising. Digestion is also weakest at night. The body goes into repair mode in the evening hours while we sleep, so it will divert energy away from digestion. Digestion requires a lot of energy. Try not to eat after 8 p.m., unless medically necessary. Also, a rule I always followed when competing in equine endurance competitions with my horse was - "No eating until relaxed and cooled down." I knew once my horse's body went into 'work and competing mode' his digestion would slow down extremely due to the stress. I would feed my horse once his body was back into a parasympathetic mode and fully capable of digestion with ease. Horses can be severely injured due to compromised digestion, which can result in colic.

Chew Your Food

Get into the habit of chewing your food thoroughly and being relaxed when you eat. Digestion starts in the mouth with saliva. Saliva contains enzymes which begin to break food down. Saliva also makes food more alkaline and easier to digest and extract nutrients from. A naturopathic doctor once put me on the 'Chew Chew diet'. It was her way of telling me I needed to chew my food instead of inhaling it! I would take a bite, chew a few times and swallow, hardly breaking the food down at all! This is what the majority of people do without realizing the damage they could be doing to their body. Now I relax and take my time eating. I try to chew at least 30 times or until the food is liquid before swallowing. It really doesn't take forever either! You'll be amazed at how this can help improve digestion. Saliva is a really important part of the digestion process.

Digestive Enzymes

Supplementing with digestive enzymes is an option if digestion is impaired. Some people benefit from a multi enzyme product, which may include proteases (break down proteins), lipase (break down fats) and carbohydrases such as amylase (break down carbohydrates).

How does a person know if they should be supplementing with digestive aids? The best way to know is probably by stool testing, to measure how well you are digesting your food and how well your pancreas is producing digestive enzymes. Seek out a qualified functional practitioner you trust to help you get this testing.

The best sources of enzymes are from foods in their raw, live or sprouted form. When purchased from a store digestive enzymes have a reputation of being very safe and reasonably inexpensive.

Look at the labels and make sure you are getting a quality product, it does make a difference. Always check ingredient labels on any supplements you buy. You especially want to pay attention to what ingredients are *not* in the product such as gluten, dairy, etc. If it doesn't say "contains no: wheat, gluten, soy, sugar, milk, egg, shellfish, salt or preservatives," you should always assume it does.

Fiber

A good source of fiber can be helpful to some people, but fiber is not always the best catalyst for regular bowel movements for people who deal with constipation. In my experience fiber can sometimes make the symptoms worse. Insoluble fiber can be problematic for some people, especially if they have SIBO (Small Intestinal Bacterial Overgrowth), it can seriously aggravate the symptoms. If you have chronic constipation (you should be moving bowels twice a day hopefully) and SIBO is suspected, your practitioner can offer a breath test and an organic acids profile to see what the results show. SIBO is a type of overgrowth in the bacteria that produces a methane gas. There can be up to a 70% reduction in mobility in the presence of methane gas. There are good treatments available for SIBO.

Fats

Fat is the number one trigger for peristalsis; or the motion of the bowels. Constipation can be the result of not having enough good fat in the diet. One of the biggest mistakes I see today is people eating tons of low fat and no fat foods thinking it's good for them. In truth, these types of "fat" are not beneficial. However, there are many different types of fats and the good fats are necessary for good health. How can you bring good fats into your diet? There are many simple ways. Add a tablespoon or two of coconut oil to a meal. Drink bone broth from healthy grass fed sources or add the bones, or already made broth to your soups. Flaxseeds are a great source of omega-3 fatty acids, grind them in a coffee grinder or small blender and add them to a smoothie. Flaxseeds have a nutty flavor; make sure you store them properly to ensure freshness. Free Range, organically grown eggs are a great source of beneficial fats, including the fat soluble vitamins A and D, as well as folic acid and the adrenal building minerals choline, potassium, sulfur and phosphorous. Eliminate trans fats, seed and vegetable oils that overwhelm your omega-6 levels. Eliminate margarine! Eliminate refined, processed low fat foods. There are healing fats and there are killing fats, research this subject further and know which ones you are eating.

Oxalates

I will make a brief mention about oxalates. In a healthy gut, oxalates are not a problem. Cabbage, nightshade vegetables, grains and more are high in oxalates, which may cause problems in people with gut inflammation or Leaky Gut. Information provided on the Great Plains Laboratory web site explains how in a healthy non-leaky gut, oxalates are broken down by the bacteria 'oxalobacter formingenes', preventing the molecules from traveling to the large intestine and being absorbed by body tissues. Blood and urine samples would show a low oxalate content. In a leaky gut when oxalobacter is lowered by antibiotics as an example, oxalates can escape out into the bloodstream causing damage to tissue, glands, secretory organs and the brain. The Great Plains Laboratory web site has some excellent literature on this subject, including an article about Autism and the inability to break down oxalates due to Candida or fungus. [15 16]

Be aware of this if you have a leaky gut or chronic inflammation. I remained on a strict elimination diet for a period of time until I saw measurable improvement. The elimination diet really wasn't hard once I got started and it helped me get out of a wheelchair! In time, I began to reintroduce foods to see which ones were contributing to the symptoms. I ended up with the knowledge of which foods were healing me and which foods caused inflammation and dysfunction. I still prefer and continue to soak nuts and grains prior to eating them. There is a great deal of information available online if you want to research oxalates further.

A few more basic tips for better digestion:

- Take a moment before you eat to acknowledge what you are grateful for with blessings or gratitude. Doing this activates the cephalic phase of digestion. Your brain signals saliva to release and this helps strengthen your digestive fire.
- Don't drink large amounts of fluid 30 minutes before and up to 1 hour after a meal. Watering down your stomach at meal time dilutes enzymes and acids responsible for digesting food. If you must drink with a meal, drink herbal tea or warm lemon water. A spicy tea with lemon or peppermint tea helps weak digestion.
- Have your largest meal at lunch and only eat as much food as you can hold in both hands in a single meal. Don't overeat. Eating too much can make digestion difficult for your body. It is one of the causes of indigestion/reflux. Eat until you are three quarters full.
- Reduce or eliminate processed foods. They are

challenging to digest and rob the body of nutrients rather than supplying them. Your body has to use its own energy and nutrient reserves to metabolize these products. Not a good situation on a daily basis.

- Avoid greasy foods. Deep-fried foods are not good for you. Foods which are dead (refined) and have no live enzymes of their own should be minimized or avoided. I usually take digestive enzymes when eating refined or cooked foods.
- Add in probiotics. Fermented foods made at home are a superb way to increase your digestive power. They aid digestion, increase stomach acidity and proper bowel flora. Probiotics can be purchased at the store, though it is more expensive. We need good bacteria to strengthen our immune systems and reduce inflammation. My favorites are sauerkraut, water kefir, coconut kefir and kimchi.
- Boost stomach acid when needed. Consult your practitioner to figure out which protocol may be best suited to you. Belching, heartburn, gas, headaches and fatigue can all be a result of low stomach acid. I will give you examples of some of the ways I've boosted my stomach acid. There are several ways to raise the levels and I always start with the gentle, simple protocols first. Boost gently by adding fresh squeezed lemon juice in your water or by adding a tablespoon of raw fermented apple cider vinegar in water every morning. I also add raw honey to my water and cider vinegar, but that may not be good for some people. Rinse teeth/mouth with water or brush teeth after lemon or vinegar water. Another way to boost stomach acid is with Betaine HCL

and Pepsin. When eating meats I typically add Betaine HCL. This is what works for me. Remember, we are all biologically diferent and you will need to figure out what works safely for you. More on HCL below.

- A short relaxing walk after meals is helpful to digestion. It can increase circulation which helps absorption and also helps the liver.
- Exercise regularly. It takes healthy muscle tone to move food through the digestive tract.
- Drink plenty of water throughout the day. The stomach needs water, especially for the health of the mucosal lining which supports the bacteria responsible for digestion and absorption of nutrients. Lack of water can cause all kinds of difficulty including memory loss, constipation, fatigue, brain fog, indigestion and more.

Digestion and Stomach Acid

It is estimated 90% of Americans have low stomach acid, called hypochlorhydria. Unfortunately society automatically assumes indigestion or reflux is caused by too much acid when research is actually showing the opposite. Low stomach acid can lead to a cascade of digestive problems such as bloating, gas and constipation. Fortunately there are natural ways to support your body's digestive system and raise levels of stomach acid.

First let's look at why sufficient levels of stomach acid (HCL) are important by asking what the consequences of low stomach acid are. If you have low stomach acid:

- Your body's defense system is lowered. HCL kills pathogens and prevents them from passing further into your body. Here's an example; in a low stomach acid environment bacteria such as H. pylori are able to reproduce, overgrow, and suppress stomach acid even further. They will create an environment favorable for their survival not yours.

- Your body will have to work much harder to digest food and separate nutrients from it. You may even have a situation when the HCL levels are so low your stomach isn't acidic enough to digest proteins. When a person is unable to properly break proteins down it leads to mal-digestion and poor body condition; hair loss and brittle nails are two examples.
- You may have difficulty breaking proteins down into amino acids. Lack of amino acids in the bloodstream may mean less available neurotransmitters which could lead to mood disorders like depression. Additionally, this allows undigested proteins, pathogens and other molecules to move into your small intestines, creating a multitude of problems.
- Nutrient absorption is hindered. When proteins aren't fully broken down, vitamin B12, folate and non-heme iron absorption are disrupted.
- You may suffer from heartburn/GERD/reflux. The Lower Esophageal Sphincter (LES) separates the esophagus and the stomach. Proper levels of stomach acid signal the LES to close tightly. If stomach acid level is low the LES loosens and acidic stomach fluid can escape into the lower part of the esophagus causing a burning sensation. LES dysfunction may also be influenced by other factors such as certain drugs, food allergies and overeating.
- You will likely suffer from constipation, bloating, gas and belching. The pyloric sphincter separates the stomach

from the small intestine. The body may resist opening this sphincter when stomach acid pH is not low enough for proper digestion. The body innately knows that undigested food will cause problems in the intestines. Without adequate acid, food will sit in the stomach and putrefy instead of being properly digested.

- You may notice undigested food particles showing up in your stool.

HCL and digestive enzymes made a huge difference for me. I've known for a number of years I was having trouble digesting heavier proteins and meat, but it took a lot of research and experimenting to understand why this might be happening.

Here's the digestive process made simple...

Most people, including me, are told they have excessive stomach acid. Taking antacids is the typical protocol and did bring some relief of the symptoms for me. But eventually I had more problems and symptoms returned. Taking the antacids helped temporarily alleviate a painful symptom but did not solve the root of the problem. I eventually learned antacids come with unpleasant side effects as do Proton Pump Inhibitors (PPI's). For me, antacids and heartburn medications contributed to a cascade of even more problems. This is why it was so important for me to correct the stomach acid problem rather than use a drug that would reduce acid further. Taking antacids, whether over the counter or prescription, is often counterproductive to healing. Do most doctors even check to verify the problem is excessive acid in the stomach prior to prescribing drugs? Not in my experience.

If you're not digesting proteins or meat well, you may have similar signs to what I had; test results may show you in the normal reference range, yet on the low side in the B vitamins, zinc, iron and other minerals. In fact, your blood panel may look like that of a vegetarian even though you're eating meat. That's a red flag. I also felt very sluggish and heavy after eating meat and it would slow my digestion contributing to constipation. Sometimes headaches would accompany this. It was so bad I stopped eating meat for many years. Eventually, I brought small amounts of meat back into my diet, but I remain mostly vegetarian and it works for me. As you start playing with, modifying, and changing around foods you eat, you will find what works for you. Always be open to the possibility that as you heal, your needs may change and vary.

What Suppresses Stomach Acid?

Adrenal fatigue, some infections, antibiotics, candida, lack of mineral reserves, there could be a methylation issue such as the MTHFR mutation just to name a few. If the stomach acid is off, everything is off. Digestion doesn't function and support the body as it was designed to. The stomach needs an acidic environment to complete its job in the digestive process. You'll have difficulty extracting and getting nutrients into the body. The closest thing to a magic pill for me has been HCL and digestive enzymes! I've used both as digestive support for my body during times of imbalance or stress when I'm less able to produce enough enzymes and HCL on my own. Dosage is dependent on what type of meal I'm eating.

When stomach acid has been chronically low for many years the lining of the stomach may be too inflamed to tolerate HCL supplementation. I found cabbage juice to be very helpful to healing the lining. Cabbage has a very powerful healing enzyme in it and is highly praised for its anti-ulcer capabilities. It can help to sooth an inflamed stomach lining as well as assist in correcting low stomach acid. I started by drinking ½ a teaspoon each day and building up as I could tolerate it. I'm careful to not overdo it because like anything, too much may cause problems by pushing too much too fast, especially in a body challenged with imbalances. Large amounts could possibly suppress a stressed thyroid due to goitrogens.

Make sure you are working with a knowledgeable practitioner if you go down this road. You don't want to take HCL if you do not need it or if you have H. pylori. You also want to make sure you have the right dose for your body. As with many things, too much could cause damage. When you digest better you will feel better. Digestive distress may be reduced. Dr. Jonathan Wright has a book called *Why Stomach Acid Is Good For You*. I highly recommend it.

My goal is always to recuperate and rebuild to the level that I can slowly wean off of the HCL and enzymes as my body is healing and able to increase its own production capacity. I supplement when necessary because digesting my food and being able to extract the nutrients is crucial to the healing process.

Because this is such an important subject I would like to share information which can be found on Dr. Jeff McCombs' web site. Dr. McCombs is the author of *Lifeforce* and *The Everything Candida Diet Book.* I do not personally know Dr. McCombs, I found him through research and obtained permission to reprint this article. Below, are his thoughts on Hydrochloric Acid and Health as written 11-5-12 on his blog located at *http://candidaplan.com*. The direct link to this article is *http://candidaplan.com/blog/699/hydrochloric-acid-and-health/*

Hydrochloric Acid and Health

Hydrochloric acid (HCL) is produced in the stomach to aid in activating digestion of foods and protection of the intestinal flora. Excess stomach acid (HCL) has traditionally been treated as a result of low HCL levels that create cycles of over- and under – production. With the advent of direct-to-consumer marketing by pharmaceutical companies, the public was entrained to believe that this was purely an excess HCL problem that needed to be suppressed with antacids, leaving behind the science, physiology, and wisdom of the body.

By suppressing HCL levels, you lose absorption of protein, iron, iodine, B12, Folic acid, Zinc, Calcium, Magnesium, and other minerals. Current antacid products started carrying a Black Box Warning in 2010 about their use leading to osteoporosis from decreased calcium absorption. Another warning about the loss of Magnesium was released in 2012 by the FDA - http://curezone.com/forums/fm.asp?i=1908229#i The Journal of the American Medical Association has now published a study at the end of 2013 that demonstrates that these medications are linked to B12 deficiencies. It has taken 20-30 years to get these Black Box warnings on these medications, when they should have been there from the beginning. This is just basic physiology, which it appears the medical profession no longer understands. Eventually, all of these losses will need to be considered, as they all occur. Black Box Warnings should read:

"Can lead to loss of absorption of Protein, Iron, Iodine, B12, Folic acid, Zinc, Calcium, Magnesium, and other vitamins and minerals leading to sickness, serious diseases, and some forms of cancer!"

You also lose the protective and functional effects that HCL provides. Proper HCL levels in the stomach kill off many pathogens that otherwise would enter into the intestinal tract and potentially create problems. Clostridium difficile, the number one cause of infectious disease deaths with over 30,000 per year, is linked to antacid medications. Proper HCL levels are necessary to digestive function once food leaves the stomach and passes into the intestinal tract. The acidic base that food is in, as well as the partially digested foods from HCL's presence in the stomach, trigger further digestion and absorption of nutrients. Without this, we don't have proper liver/gallbladder and pancreatic function and digestion. This will cause further nutritional losses of fats, fat-soluble vitamins, proteins, etc.

HCL deficiencies can lead to the creation and overgrowth of pathogenic bacteria and fungus in the intestinal tract through altered pH. The downside to HCL deficiency spirals out exponentially at a very rapid pace creating systemic problems throughout the body and contributing to long-term health challenges, conditions, and diseases.

*A recent study found that 71% of patients taking antacid medication, Proton Pump Inhibitors (**Tagamet, Zantac, Aciphex, Protonix, and Nexium**) or H2 Receptor antagonists (**Tagamet, Zantac, Ranitidine**) had fungal candida overgrowth. Also present, was overgrowth of antibiotic resistant strains of bacteria. Both findings point to the lasting effects of antibiotics in the body, and the risk of antacid medications. Prolonged use of antacid medications is associated with increased risk of hypergastrinaemia that leads to cancer. Taking antacid medications causes destruction of the stomach lining.*

Low HCL levels are associated with skin conditions such as psoriasis, eczema, rosacea, boils and dermatitis, as well as problems like fibromyalgia.

One of the most common causes of HCL imbalances is past antibiotic use. Antibiotics destroy the beneficial bacteria that synthesize B vitamins necessary for HCL production in the stomach. Antibiotics alone are not shown to be capable of inducing low levels of HCL. It also requires the overgrowth of fungal candida that happens subsequent to antibiotic use. Fungal candida plays a role in reshaping the bacterial flora to a composition that affects HCL production.

It is believed that HCL production starts to decline as we get older. This may also be a result of past antibiotic use, so I'm not as convinced that this is a normal part of aging, as it is a normal part of society that is over-inundated with antibiotic exposures. Once antibiotics destroy the beneficial bacteria of the stomach and intestines, candida plays a role in determining subsequent function.

Unfortunately, most medical doctors are completely unaware of the widespread nutritional and functional downside from antibiotic and antacid use. If you'd like to put your MD through the litmus test on his knowledge of human physiology, a required course of study for all doctors in order to be licensed, ask him to explain which nutrients are lost when taking antacid medications. Then observe as all kinds of responses manifest, except a direct answer to your question. Ask him to give you the typical dosage on antacid medications and he'll pass with flying colors. The knowledge of the human body has been replaced with pharmaceutical protocols.

Many Holistic doctors treat low HCL by giving Betaine HCL with Pepsin in either capsule or tablet form. If someone has chronic inflammation of the intestinal tract and they take HCL, it tends to produce a burning sensation. A warming sensation is normal. A burning sensation with just one capsule can be diagnostic for chronic intestinal inflammation. In either case, restoring normal HCL levels is essential to health, and chronic low levels can have a tremendous negative effect on health and healing.

The typical protocol for taking HCL is as follows:

You start by taking 1 capsule of HCL with each meal. If no burning occurs, continue to increase this by 1 with each meal, per day, or every other day, until it creates a burning sensation, then decrease the dosage by 1 capsule and stay at this dosage. For example, you take 1 capsule with each meal on Monday. If no burning, take 2 capsules with each meal on Wednesday. If no burning, take 3 capsules with each meal on Friday, etc. Now if on Saturday, you took 4 capsules and experienced a burning sensation, then you would back off to the 3 capsules with each meal and stay at that dosage. Some people get up to 4-8 capsules with each meal. How long you stay there varies, but I have seen some people do this for a year or two, before they start to get a burning sensation and then need to reduce the dosage. Once in a great while, someone will do the 1 pill with each meal for one day and then find that their HCL production kicks in and they don't need it any more. It's a rarity, but does happen. Balancing your digestive function at the same time through the McCombs Plan can help to reduce how long someone might need to take HCL.

So how do you know if you have a HCL deficiency? The expensive way is via the Heidelberg pH Capsule or the Gastrocap. This is ordered by your doctor. Another way to check at home is to mix one-quarter teaspoon of baking soda in eight ounces of cold water, first thing in the morning, before eating or drinking anything except water. Drink the baking soda solution. Time how long it takes to belch. Time up to five minutes. If you have not belched within five minutes stop timing anyway.

If your stomach is producing adequate amounts of hydrochloric acid you should probably belch within two to three minutes. Three to five minutes will most likely be due to some level of deficiency. Early and repeated belching may be due to excessive stomach acid. Belching results from the acid and baking soda reacting to form carbon dioxide gas. The Heidelberg or Gastrocap tests can be employed for confirmation of the results of this test.

If while you're correcting HCL imbalances, you find that you have an excess amount at any time, the old remedy of ¼ teaspoon of baking soda in some water works well. Antacid medications can continue to produce negative effects years after discontinuing them.

For those people who find themselves caught in the cycle of chronic intestinal inflammation and HCL imbalances and taking 1 capsule produces burning, you may have to start by opening the HCL capsule and using just a pinch of HCL with each meal mixed in water. It can be a bit of an uphill battle, but it is a much better alternative to a steady downhill slide in overall health. For long-lasting results, restoring the health of the digestive tract will produce the best results.

The bottom line is this: Antibiotic use and subsequent fungal candida overgrowth together can create low levels of HCL that lead to acid reflux, gastritis, ulcers, and a number of conditions. Treatment with antacid medications helps to create even more fungal candida overgrowth and a very long list of conditions, diseases, and cancers. Either way, fungal candida will be present. How will you treat it?

All sources are linked to this article on Dr. McCombs' blog for further research and confirmation. The direct link is:

http://candidaplan.com/blog/699/hydrochloric-acid-and-health/

8
THE WHAT & WHY OF CLEANSING

Of course we're all going to die sometime, but must it be so full of pain? Being incapacitated due to stroke, heart attack, neurologic disease, or horrible pain from diabetic neuropathy or chemo treatments for cancer are in my opinion a fate worse than death. I'll take lifestyle change and better quality of life any day.

There are four basic body processes

1. Digestion
2. Absorption
3. Utilization of Minerals and Nutrients
4. Elimination

Your body wants to be healthy. It wants to cleanse and remove the garbage. Think of it like this: In your home you must take out the garbage to keep the house fresh and clean. Cleansing is about taking out your internal garbage so your body can properly digest, absorb, utilize, and eliminate. The resulting effect is a feeling of endless energy along with a rebooted metabolism.

When the body is toxic it cannot properly perform its functions. Your digestive tract and intestines are responsible for the absorption of all of your food's nutrients, amino acids and minerals. A healthy cleanse can assist you in removing your trash and ridding your body of stored toxins which could be inhibiting good health. The elimination of unwanted toxins allows your body to thrive on a cellular level. Getting digestion working optimally is key to making this happen. Reducing toxins and cleansing on a cellular level are important to a life of good health and ease.

Cleansing is necessary to be healthy and free of ailments. We live and breathe toxicity daily. Look around you and at the world we live in. Look at the personal products you use, the paint on the walls, carpets on the floor, cleaning products in your bathroom. Most of these common items release chemicals and toxins into the air or in your body. We are constantly around chemicals and toxins. This is why it's crucial that your body is able to easily process and eliminate its trash on a regular basis. There are many ways to detox and cleanse. One of my favorites is with a sauna, but not just any sauna. I purchased a Far Infrared Sauna more than 7 years ago and regard it as one of the smartest things I've done for myself. I highly recommend this type of sauna for regular easy cleansing. Be sure if you purchase a sauna that it's not constructed with toxic products. You can find a link to the sauna I personally use on my web site if you're interested. Choosing to cleanse is a positive choice to help your body to perform its job of keeping you healthy. I have found it's important to keep it simple and start slow.

Elimination diets are a another wonderful way to cleanse. If you have never done an elimination diet or cleanse, I would suggest you seek the guidance of an experienced practitioner (includes Nutrition (FDN), Health Coach or others) the first time. It's very helpful to utilize a cleanse program that has a guide book, preparation material, meal planning tips, recipes and a lot of great educational information on cleansing. This makes it easy!

I prefer to follow seasonal cleansing using the Chinese Five Element System. Why? Because according to Traditional Chinese Medicine which has been successfully practiced for thousands of years, energy in your body concentrates to a specific set of organs during a specific season, like spring or fall. You are probably familiar with maintaining your car by the seasons, right? You may change oil seasonally or have antifreeze checked and flushed or winter tires put on seasonally. Your body needs the same kind of maintenance.

Let me give you an example. In Chinese medicine Spring is connected to the liver and the gallbladder. These two organs are blood cleansers and they both work hard to keep your body free of toxins. In Western medicine the liver is also associated with detoxification and blood filtration. Its job is to filter and neutralize the harmful substances in your body so they don't do any damage. When there is toxic buildup in the liver and gallbladder the body can start to experience physical reactions such as exhaustion, colds, weight gain and depression, to name a few.

The liver wakes up in the spring and when imbalances exist in the body it's not uncommon to experience feelings of anger, headaches, rashes and/or sleepless nights during this season. With over 500 metabolic processes, the liver is the 'Master Detox Organ' of the body. When the liver is congested your digestion is impaired, which results in a toxic overload. In honoring the spring season, the goal is to cleanse the liver and improve its ability to function. Choosing the right foods to heal the body and support proper detoxification by the liver cleanses the liver for a fresh and harmonious body.

This is why I try to eat and cleanse with the seasons, it supports detoxification and is fairly easy because I grow a lot of my food. Spring brings with it wonderful dark leafy greens like spinach, Swiss chard, and kale. It also brings dandelion, nettles,

asparagus, and peas. All are wonderful choices for the liver. Each season has its own special focus for cleansing. Here is the calendar:

Winter – December 21	Nourish Kidneys and Urinary Bladder
Late Winter	Cleanse Liver and Gall Bladder
Spring – March 21	Nourish Liver and Gall Bladder
Late Spring	Cleanse Intestinal System
Mid Summer – June 21	Nourish Heart and Small Intestine
Late Summer	Nourish Spleen, Pancreas, Stomach and Cleanse Lungs
Fall – September 21	Nourish Lungs and Small Intestines
Late Fall	Cleanse Kidneys

Every season has a different feel and focus. Another brief example is summer. Trees are blooming, seasonal fruits are juicy, ripe and delicious and the season is warm and packed with fun activities. This season encourages you to lighten up and feel free. In the summer the body naturally wants to cool off and eat lighter. This is the best time to eat cooling foods and make it fun! Winter brings warming foods and so on.

The Five Element system says you are to nourish the organs during the corresponding season. An example would be taking herbs, which support the kidneys during the winter season. Toward the end of the season, just before the next season begins, you cleanse the organs that correspond to the upcoming season.

The organ energies also follow an internal clock.

- 7 – 9 a.m. Stomach
- 9 – 11 a.m. Spleen
- 11 – 1 p.m. Heart

- 1 – 3 p.m. Small Intestines
- 3 – 5 p.m. Bladder
- 5 – 7 p.m. Kidneys
- 7 – 9 p.m. Pericardium
- 9 – 11 p.m. Triple Energizer
- 11 – 1 a.m. Gall Bladder
- 1 – 3 a.m. Liver
- 3 – 5 a.m. Lungs
- 5 – 7 a.m. Large Intestines

There are wonderful books available that go deeper into the Five Element system and Traditional Chinese Medicine (TCM). It's a lot of fun to explore and learn.

Digestion and Cleansing

The digestive system can become weakened or damaged by the foods we eat and the toxins we take in. Poor digestion can lead to toxic overload in the liver, lymphatic system and kidneys, which leads to inflammation and more disease and illness. Cleansing with an elimination diet for a week can help to support your body to remove toxins and reduce inflammation by reducing your intake of certain foods possibly wreaking havoc on your body and hampering your digestive fire. After the week is over, you re-introduce the foods that possibly caused inflammation one at a time and watch for reactions. A food journal is really helpful. Journaling provides clarity by defining which foods make you feel good and which ones cause reactions such as bloating, gas, constipation/diarrhea, weight gain, acne, headaches, reflux or heartburn. The goal of cleansing is to reset, recharge, and rejuvenate your body.

People are confused about what to eat. One day you're told eggs are bad and the next they're good. Choices are based upon foods that are popularly considered to be healthy and people are still not getting the results they want. The problem with cookie cutter guidance is that some of the foods may not be good for your unique body. Foods such as grains, corn, eggs, dairy and sugar are all commonly known to cause allergies, sensitivities, digestive problems, moodiness, hormonal issues, infertility and inflammation in some people. A cleanse using an elimination diet will allow you to find out what works for YOU. Removing foods which often cause negative reactions as discussed above and later reintroducing them to your diet allows greater insight into your own body. You will be empowered to choose foods that give you fuel and avoid the foods that do not!

I'm going to end this chapter with one of the recipes from my Re-Boot Your Body cleanse available on *www.cultivatinghealth.org*. This is one of my favorite smoothies, especially when I'm craving chocolate. It's healthy and tastes amazing! I hope you enjoy it.

Chocolate Fantasy Smoothie

1 cup	milk; unsweetened almond, coconut, hemp, rice milk or raw milk
1	ripe banana
2 Tbs	sun butter
1 Tbs	raw honey or stevia
2 Tbs	raw cacao or unsweetened cocoa powder
	ice optional

9
SIGNIFICANT OTHERS IN YOUR LIFE

We think we know so much, yet in reality we know so little.

Hormones

It is impossible to achieve optimum health without a properly functioning hormonal system. Proper function and balance of hormone metabolic pathways is critical. If anything is off, everything is off. There is a ripple effect, just as when you toss a pebble into a pond and the ripple flows all the way through the body of water. Hormonal balance affects all other function in your body. Organs and systems such as thyroid, adrenals, pancreas, liver, blood sugar regulation, cell energy production and much more will function poorly if there is an imbalance. Your body is designed to handle certain stressors; it will adapt. Constant stress and other factors in our lives today are contributing to an epidemic of hormonal disruption and adrenal dysfunction. For the hormone system to be working all of the endocrine glands (thyroid, pituitary, adrenals, testes and ovaries) must function optimally.

The adrenal glands sit on top of the kidneys and release hormones in response to stress which allows a person to adapt to changes in the environment. They are often referred to as the 'fight or flight' glands and are responsible for the 'rush' needed to flee or fight. The adrenal gland response to anger, fear and panic can include increases in blood pressure, mobilization of sugar from the liver to the blood stream and increased heart rate. These are vital to a successful fight or flight reaction.

If your adrenals are in good health, you can handle stress better and for longer periods of time. The adrenal glands produce many hormones including; cortisol (hydrocortisone), adrenalin (epinephrine), DHEA, pregnenolone, progesterone, estrogen and testosterone. If you are under stress the adrenal glands will keep producing cortisol to help you adapt. If this continues for a long time or becomes chronic the adrenal glands will become exhausted and unable to continue producing that same level of cortisol. You will begin to feel different when this happens. Kind of like staying on a bicycle too long, you feel it when you've gone past your limit.

In early adrenal fatigue people usually still feel good because the body is still adapting and able to pump out the cortisol. You many not feel as good as you used to or you may feel tired and wired, but you can keep on going. It is possible to remain this way for years before advancing to further stages of adrenal dysfunction or you could quickly advance. It depends on the individual and their circumstances.

As you move into more advanced stages of adrenal dysfunction your body will not adapt as it did previously and cortisol output will diminish. Hormones will be out of balance and you will feel it. Resistance to disease will be lowered, aches and pains can become more prominent and sleep may be disrupted. Your doctor may say everything looks normal. Many people begin using supplements and medications to try to feel better, yet don't understand what is going on.

When this happened to me many years ago I definitely had no clue what was going on within my body. It was eventually revealed I was in full blown adrenal failure! My body was barely producing cortisol compared to what a healthy person would. Cortisol levels were extremely low when they should be high and high when they should have been low. My circadian rhythm was really messed up. No wonder I couldn't sleep at night and was always so exhausted, achy, and in pain! Pieces of the endocrine puzzle had been partially looked at, but the understanding and focus of the entire picture and root cause had been missing.

Through my research I found cortisol to be one of the main anti-inflammatory hormones. I was fascinated by this because my production of cortisol was desperately low and I suspected much of the pain I had been dealing with was likely due to uncontrolled inflammation. The information I was learning about cortisol and its effect on everything had the possibility of changing my life for the better. I had been eating the right foods, doing everything I possibly knew to promote healing, yet still couldn't seem to reduce the inflammation to allow a better quality of life. This gave me renewed hope because I learned when low cortisol levels are present, it is next to impossible to control inflammation and pain. With adrenal support and healing, maybe I could reduce pain levels along with other symptoms and rebuild health.

The number of people being tested and treated is increasing, as more and more functional nutrition practitioners and doctors become aware of the cortisol connection. It's interesting to see the results, and also unfortunate though most practitioners will see a test result within 'normal' ranges and automatically assume it means adrenals are fine. They don't know what they don't know. Fortunately there's a movement of nutritional practitioners

(FDN) being trained who do understand how to interpret findings and comprehend what may be going on at the cellular level. Many people have some level of adrenal dysfunction accompanying illness. The majority of people with serious illness and digestive difficulties seem to be showing up with gut infections, gut dysbiosis, gut permeability and severe adrenal fatigue.

What could be causing all of this? It's usually not one thing, but instead a whole bunch of things mixed together:

- Emotional stressors; an abusive spouse, death of a parent or other family member, childhood trauma, a stressful job.
- Possible hidden stressors; gluten sensitivity, allergies, toxins in the food we eat and water we drink, lack of nutrients in the food, the inability to absorb nutrients in the gut, over-exercising, parasitic or bacterial infections or candida infection.

If you have a water pitcher and the pitcher is full of water, you have to stop adding water to it or it will spill over and make a mess. When you get symptoms of disease or illness, your water pitcher has spilled over. Something has to change in your life so you can stop overfilling the pitcher. Maybe it will be a change in diet, lifestyle, job, or in your relationship status. Dealing with and reducing stress in your life is a step in the right direction.

Low cortisol levels and adrenal exhaustion may manifest symptoms such as joint pain, muscle aches, sleep dysfunction, allergies and sensitivities, hypoglycemia, sugar cravings, low blood pressure, depression, cold extremities, inflammatory bowel disease, gastritis and more. Once people get out of adrenal fatigue, are eating the foods right for their body, and clear any infections, they have an opportunity to really soar with their health.

The gut and adrenals go hand in hand. When healing one, you must not forget to support and heal the other. If you are supporting adrenals and not paying attention to gut healing it's kind of like building a castle on shifting sands. You have to rebuild the gut and the microbiome to get the foundation to support the adrenals to heal and maintain optimal function. The adrenals will then support the gut to heal and maintain optimal function. Without a foundation the sands can easily shift, allowing the castle to crumble. We are all unique and our bodies will respond differently, so there's really not a cookie cutter step-by-step formula which works for everyone. There are causal factors that can be investigated through functional lab testing which will help to determine what the path to healing or maintaining good health will look like for each of us. Following functional nutrition protocols to reset metabolic pathways can assist in healing and building strength back in the body.

While focusing on adrenals and healing over the years I have dealt with plenty of confusion and frustration. There are very few practitioners who really understand the testing and how to regain function. As I mentioned earlier, most are simply treating symptoms and not addressing the cause. In my case detox capacity, liver congestion and dysfunction were not addressed. Gut inflammation, dysbiosis and permeability were not addressed. Delayed food allergies and sensitivities were not addressed. Because of these issues I would continually go back and forth between different stages of adrenal dysfunction. My body was not prepared to handle the stress of protocols. I have found this is common in people with extreme adrenal exhaustion. I had to work to find a balance my body could succeed with. The candida and heavy metals were a daily stressor for me and I wanted to reduce that stressor so I could heal, but the caveat was I didn't have the cortisol levels and adrenal function which would support me. My body wasn't ready for that fight yet. It's kind of like training for a marathon, I had to build up to it. Logically it made sense for me to start removing the heavy metals and candida, (the daily stressors) etc, but I learned that I also had to focus on supporting and rebuilding the adrenals and detox organs to be able to function during this process. Keep in mind that if you try a protocol with your practitioner and it causes symptoms to increase or flare, your body may be telling you that you need to build up support first. Don't lose hope! Just pay attention to what your body is telling you. The situation you are trying to heal has likely been going on for a while and you just need to be patient with yourself. Work with your practitioner to use an adrenal protocol for a few months and then re-evaluate and try again. Bringing your natural cortisol levels back into balance will make a huge difference in your ability to heal.

Cortisol impacts over 2000 epigenetic on and off switches for the immune system each and every day! Think about that, it's huge. Once you start to bring your cortisol and hormone levels into balance, you will feel a difference. You will start feeling better and having more energy. When you start to get some of your energy back, you are more prepared for the fight with candida, heavy metals, bacteria or parasites. You can come in with the protocol and kill the infections, or remove heavy metals (the stressors) and then you can really take off like a rocket and experience higher levels of energy and feel much better.

In my situation, I've had to do it in layers. There were a multitude of stressors and as I dealt with one, it allowed me to heal a little. I would then address the next and it allowed another level of healing and so on. I have learned to reduce stress, stand up for myself, have more fun in life, prioritize self care and eat well. It's been like a puzzle and I continue to be amazed at the process and the progress. I have also learned we are all sort of like snowflakes, unique in our own way. What works for one may not work for another, but the principle is similar.

Is My Thyroid Making My Butt Look Big?

The thyroid gland is a butterfly shaped gland located in the lower part of the neck. It is responsible for many crucial functions in your body. Every cell in the body has receptors for thyroid hormone. The thyroid hormone acts as the body's metabolic regulator and every cell, muscle, and organ in the body depends on adequate amounts of thyroid hormone to attain optimal function. Thyroid hormone impacts all major systems in our body and directly impacts the brain, the cardiovascular and gastrointestinal systems, gall bladder and liver function, glucose metabolism, bone metabolism, lipid and cholesterol metabolism, protein metabolism and body temperature regulation. I'm sure there are more things I haven't listed, but you get the picture right?

A cog on a wheel has a series of projections on its edge that transfers motion by engaging with projections on another wheel which is central to everything running properly. The thyroid, a major gland in maintaining health is kind of like a cog. This gland secretes approximately one teaspoon of thyroid hormone in a year. This small amount of hormone is what drives the metabolic rate of your cells. Any small deviation could bring great consequences for your health.

When the thyroid gland is not producing enough hormone it is labeled as hypothyroidism. Some signs of **hypo**thyroidism are:

- Elevated cholesterol
- Fatigue
- Infertility, menstrual irregularities
- Mental slowness or inability to concentrate

- Cold intolerance, cold hands and feet
- Depression, irritability, nervousness
- Dementia, poor memory
- Weight gain, puffy eyes, eyelid swelling
- Hair thinning or loss, brittle nails, dry skin
- Constipation
- Muscle cramps, muscle stiffness, muscle weakness
- Hypotension or essential hypertension
- Difficulty swallowing, throat pain, hoarse voice
- Slower heartbeat

When the thyroid gland is producing too much hormone it is labeled as hyperthyroidism. Some signs of **hyper**thyroidism are:

- Fatigue
- Goiter
- Heat intolerance
- Hyperactivity
- Hypertension
- Menstrual disturbances
- Palpitations
- Eye disorders
- Weight loss
- Nerve tingling
- Increased appetite
- Nervousness, sweating
- Tremors, weakness

Thyroid disease is often under diagnosed and misdiagnosed. The majority of doctors rely on blood testing alone to diagnose a thyroid condition, only looking at the TSH and T4. This is so unfortunate. The doctor may tell you your thyroid tests are normal because to them it looks normal. They haven't been trained to test and look at all of the functions and processes involved, especially at the cellular level. Therefore, they neither "see" what is going on, nor understand how to address the underlying mechanisms involved. Then one day you wake up and are told the damage is so great you must remove the thyroid completely. Something is missing and opportunities for healing are being lost.

Studies show 90% of people with hypothyroidism are producing antibodies to thyroid tissue.[17] I used to be one of those 90%, but thankfully no longer belong in that group. Graves' disease and Hashimoto's disease are two examples of autoimmune disorders of the thyroid gland. In Hashimoto's and Graves' the body produces antibody's which attack its own thyroid gland. The antibodies will attach to cells on the thyroid causing inflammation and frequently destruction of the thyroid. As the thyroid becomes more inflamed it may release too much hormone causing signs of hyperthyroid. Autoimmune thyroid problems can lead to **hyper**thyroidism initially, which may then be followed by **hypo**thyroidism later in the illness. Most doctors recognize the connection between thyroid disorders and autoimmune disease. Most patients don't understand the connection because doctors don't always tell the patient because they don't have the time and it doesn't change the treatment plan.

Conventional medicine doesn't seem to have an effective plan for autoimmune disease. They use steroids and other synthetic medications to suppress the immune system. It is now believed in the case of Hashimoto's the consequences (side effects and complications of immunosuppressive drugs) outweigh the potential benefits. I agree because that was my experience. I learned it is also fairly usual for Hashimoto's patients to have antibodies to other tissues as well. The most common are reported to be transglutaminase (Celiac disease), the cerebellum (neurological disorders), intrinsic factor (pernicious anemia), glutamic acid decarboxylase (anxiety/panic attacks and late onset type 1 diabetes).

Generally speaking, the Hashimoto's patient is sent home to wait until the immune system has caused enough damage to the thyroid tissue to categorize them as hypothyroid. They will then be prescribed a thyroid hormone replacement. If they show up with other symptoms such as insulin resistance or depression they'll be prescribed drugs for that too. In these situations no one is bothering to look for the underlying cause of the immune system attacking the thyroid. If underlying causes are ignored, treatment isn't going to be very effective and the condition could worsen with time. Eventually surgery may be needed. What should be acknowledged is the problem may not be entirely with the thyroid; it might be a problem of the immune system attacking the thyroid. Understanding this is vital. **The entire body is affected when you are dealing with autoimmunity, not just the thyroid.** The type of care currently given for thyroid disorders is totally inadequate in my opinion.

An estimated 20 million Americans have some sort of thyroid disorder and more than half are unaware of their condition. This is not just a problem in the United States, it's a global problem. Other statistics tout 1 in 8 women will develop a thyroid disorder during her lifetime. I think this number may be increasing. I met five people with thyroidectomy due to thyroid disease this past year. This doesn't include a friend I've known since high school who recently underwent thyroid surgery. I had only known of one person my entire life that had undergone thyroid removal surgery. Suddenly, I know more than five? All five had their thyroids removed within the last three years. Wow, what's going on?

One of the biggest challenges for me has been getting my thyroid and adrenals back to a healthier state. I always have to refer to what I call my "mechanics state of mind" when I feel things changing. As I mentioned earlier, I was blessed that my doctor ran a complete thyroid panel and we were aware long ago of the autoimmune component. The problem was the only treatment offered was the drug Synthroid. I was tested for antibodies, which would indicate celiac disease or gluten intolerance and the tests came back negative. Because of this I was told I didn't have any issues with gluten and I could keep on eating it. In time, I did figure out on my own , that gluten was indeed a problem for me and I removed it from my diet.

I was on Synthroid for over 10 years, and eventually was able to wean off of it and discontinue its use. I am not suggesting you discontinue use of Synthroid or any thyroid hormone. I am not against a pharmaceutical approach to thyroid hormone if it works for someone. There are also natural non-drug versions available. Thyroid hormones are so important for proper body function, you don't want to simply stop using them or ignore the malfunction. I am doing what works for my body and we are all different. I continue to utilize other types of support for my thyroid. Other types of support might include quality glandulars (freeze-dried tablets or capsules containing defatted organs, glands, or other tissue from bovine or porcine sources), adaptogens (plant compounds/herbals) and the recognition of the connection between the thyroid, the gut, hormones and the rest of my body, which I talk about throughout this book. Blood sugar imbalances and poor gut health can lead to hypothyroidism and Hashimoto's. The harmful effects of adrenal stress can seal the deal. Are these the only causes? Probably not, but they are certainly some to be aware of.

Point is: if you have symptoms consistent with hypo or hyperthyroid and suspect disease, find a doctor who understands functional medicine or a functional nutrition practitioner. Find someone who will look for the cause and get the help you need without delay. Just because you've been told your thyroid tests are in the normal range does not necessarily mean everything's fine. There's much more to thyroid function than TSH (Thyroid Stimulating Hormone) and T4.

Here are some tips I have learned over the years:

- Subclinical hypothyroidism is widespread. If you have trouble losing unexplained weight or have unexplained low energy or other important symptoms find a doctor who will run a full thyroid test panel. It's called a Comprehensive Thyroid Panel and should include TSH (Thyroid Stimulating Hormone), TSH free, T4 (Thyroxine) total, T4 free, T3 (Triiodothyronine) total, T3 free, T3 uptake, T3 reverse, both (TG) Thyroglobulin AB and (TPO) Thyroid peroxidase AB (auto-antibodies).
- The thyroid can really respond to toxicity. If you are not dealing with autoimmunity and adrenals are in good shape, look for toxicities. Your liver may need to be cleansed.
- A thyroid hormone prescription may not work well if you are a poor T4 to T3 converter. You may need a compounded blend or a natural thyroid extract. If thyroid hormone makes you jittery as it did me at times, adrenals could be an issue.
- T4 to T3 conversion needs selenium and iron. Levels of RBC selenium and feritin can be tested. You may need to supplement with selenium. A few brazil nuts per day is a safe and easy way to start getting selenium into the

body.

- Adrenals should be tested using a 4 sample saliva test spread over a single day. Just because an adrenal test shows you are within a normal range doesn't necessarily mean things are fine. An FDN (Functional Diagnostic Nutrition) practitioner is trained in interpreting the test results, you may want to locate one at: *http://functionaldiagnosticnutrition.com/practitioners/*

- Above all else, start eating real, whole, and nutrient-rich healthy foods!

Here is a list of some of the things that can go wrong if thyroid hormones are low:

- Blood sugar imbalances, weight gain
- Intestinal inflammation
- Vascular and arterial plaquing
- Decreased bone quality and increase in fractures
- Decreased energy production and metabolism in all cells
- Cholesterol elevation
- Impaired phase II detoxification
- Decreased stomach acid production
- Constipation, intestinal dysbiosis, malabsorption
- Gall stone formation
- Anemia, hair loss, dry skin, cold hands & feet
- Weakened immune system
- Reproductive dysfunction and infertility

Alkalinity and Acidity

Understanding pH and how alkalinity and acidity affect the body are very important in the healing process. You can test your body's urine and saliva pH easily at home using test strips that are sold online and in health food stores. Please note that these strips are not as precise as a lab test would be and do not take the place of lab testing. They are convenient for simple monitoring to see how something like food is affecting you. I use the test strips to help keep an eye on things especially when I'm adjusting my diet.

Alkalinity is a measure of the buffering capacity of water and its ability to resist sudden changes in pH. PH is a measure of the acidity or alkalinity of water. A neutral pH is in the center of the scale at 7.0. Anything below 7.0 is considered acidic, anything above 7.0 is considered alkaline. The scale goes from 1 to 14. If you were talking about the pipes in your home, a pH of less than 6.5 might contribute to corrosion and breakdown of the pipe. I have to wonder what effect a low pH might have on my body parts that aren't supposed to be in an acidic environment. I'm not sure, but I doubt it's really good.

Each of your body fluids has a different pH. Your stomach acid has a very low pH. Whereas, your saliva and bile are alkaline. Your body's enzymes that are crucial to important functions are affected by pH. Let me give you an example of different fluids:

- Stomach acid 1.5
- Saliva 7.1
- Blood 7.4
- Pancreatic 8.8

Urine pH fluctuates depending on what type of meal was eaten and what the body is eliminating. The pH of the blood is the most prioritized by the body. It must remain in the 7.35 – 7.45 range to sustain life.

Do you remember the basic science project of making a volcano that we all had to do in school? We used vinegar (acidic) and baking soda (alkaline) and combined the two together to get a reaction. The volcano bubbled and foamed up. When the reaction was complete you no longer had vinegar and baking soda, you had the byproducts; carbon dioxide, water, and minerals and the pH was neutral. What was learned from that project? We learned that minerals neutralize acids! This is why it's so important to be able to digest, absorb and build mineral levels in your body.

Your body has a buffering system that consists of minerals. It is your mineral reserve system. When your body becomes too acidic it can access these minerals to buffer without having to strip minerals from your largest mineral stash, your bones. If you have very little mineral reserves guess what may happen? Your body will do whatever it needs to do in order to balance, which may mean taking minerals from teeth and bones, and making your body weak.

There are many things that can cause acidity in the body, including foods, beverages, heavy metals, infections, parasites, stress and more. I won't go into this subject in depth because there are plenty of good books and articles already written about it. Do your own research and learn just how important it is to understand what your body is telling you.

Metabolic Syndrome

Doctors are told to look for an expanding waistline when diagnosing Metabolic Syndrome. If you're overweight, you may have it and you could be at a higher risk for having a heart attack or becoming diabetic. Basically, your body is actively ignoring the action of the hormone insulin. This is called insulin resistance. Let me explain briefly how it works.

You secrete insulin in response to the foods you eat to keep blood sugar under control after a meal. I mentioned earlier cortisol also plays a part in blood sugar control. When your cells are resistant to insulin your pancreas has to respond by working harder to pump out more and more insulin. Eventually the pancreas can no longer keep up with the demand and may become exhausted. Blood sugar rises out of control and you've got diabetes.

There are some people who will be insulin resistant and yet their body will be able to secrete just enough insulin to overcome, or allow things to progress very slowly over many years. Having chronically elevated insulin levels can be very harmful. Triglyceride levels, blood pressure and low levels of HDL ("the good") cholesterol may affect the individual including worsening insulin resistance. Heart disease is one of the first things that comes to mind.

What triggers metabolic syndrome? What is causing the initial insulin resistance? There are many hypotheses and what many researchers are looking at is the correlation between liver fat and insulin resistance in patients. The correlation in lean and obese patients is apparently very strong according to research being done at Yale School of Medicine.

What causes the liver to become fatty? Fatty liver is seen in both lean and obese people. Stanford University did studies with rats and found that if you want to cause insulin resistance in rats, feed them a diet of mostly fructose. (Info on *pubmed, sciencedaily.com* and more) Researchers have confirmed this finding over and over in many studies. Researchers at Colorado State University found changes in the liver could happen quickly, in a week if the animals are fed 60 or 70% sugar or fructose. When they stopped feeding them sugar and fructose, the fatty liver promptly went away and with it the insulin resistance. Similar effects have been shown in humans, though the studies were typically done with only moderate levels of fructose. Despite the research that has been accumulated, the evidence is criticized because rodents may not be the same as humans and the human studies didn't utilize fructose and glucose together. A study located on *www.ncbi.nlm.nih.gov/pubmed/2293343* titled "*Moderate amounts of fructose consumption impair insulin sensitivity in healthy young men: a randomized controlled trial*" concludes, *"this study clearly shows that moderate amounts of fructose and sucrose significantly alter hepatic insulin sensitivity and lipid metabolism compared with similar amounts of glucose."*

With all of this in mind, what is the probability metabolic syndrome can be reversed or prevented? I would suggest probability is very high with a diet low in sugar and elimination of products like high fructose corn syrup. I've seen so many cases of insulin resistance controlled easily by simple diet changes. I have controlled it this way for over 25 years. You may want to recognize you have a choice here – you can choose to remove these types of foods from your diet. Have no fear, there are still plenty of delicious foods to eat!

Is there a connection between insulin resistance and other diseases? Is insulin resistance one of the underlying problems that causes obesity, diabetes, and cancer? This would go along with the well accepted idea that many cancers are caused by the Western diet and lifestyle. Death rates from cancer, as well as those from diabetes have increased significantly in the last 60 years. Researchers recognize that many types of human cancer cells become dependent on insulin to provide the fuel for it to grow. The more insulin available, the more cancer cells can grow. So if you have insulin resistance you may be creating a great environment for cancer cells to thrive. Most of the research will attempt to find a drug that will suppress insulin signals. That may help, but would it not be easier and less expensive to prevent the problem before it escalates?

Cholesterol

The medical model says if a person has what is defined as abnormally high cholesterol, this person should be prescribed a statin drug, which are a class of drugs used to lower cholesterol levels by inhibiting the enzyme HMG-CoA reductase. They help to bring cholesterol levels down. This is currently the standard most doctors follow. There is no investigation of why the cholesterol is high in the first place. Is your body suddenly deficient of a statin drug? I don't think it can be since statin medications have never been in the human body until recent years. So what is causing the elevation of cholesterol? The definition of what a high cholesterol level is has changed many times over the years, so do we even know what numbers are truly high? What about bio-individuality, should we all have the exact same numbers? Isn't it worth investigating? For the sake of education, let's look at what statins do on a very basic level.

Statin drugs inhibit an enzyme involved in the body's production of cholesterol, especially in the liver. This decreases cholesterol production. Decreased cholesterol production leads to lower levels of the master steroid hormone pregnenolone. You need pregnenolone to manufacture other hormones to stay healthy and fully functional. Statins can have a negative impact on our steroid hormone levels. [18]

Elevated cholesterol levels are often associated with adrenal dysfunction. Yet, this isn't really looked at before prescribing statin drugs to a patient. When a person is under stress, catecholamines, which are hormones made by your adrenals and include neurotransmitters like the excitatory dopamine, nor-epinephrine and epinephrine, can cause an increased release of fatty acids into your bloodstream. Elevated cholesterol and other blood lipids increase with stress. The statin medication is not doing anything to address the underlying causal factors or helping us to be healthy. It's simply poisoning an enzyme according to many doctors I've spoken with.

Cholesterol has gotten a bad rap and statin drugs seem to be handed out like candy with no thought to the possible damage they can do. There is a long list of possible side effects from statins, and people don't seem to take them seriously. Seriously look at the insert that comes with pills you've been prescribed. Listen to the legal disclaimers at the end of a pharmaceutical drug advertisement. You might be thinking, "That won't happen to me." But, what if it does? It happened to somebody or it wouldn't be considered a risk would it? The web sites *www.Mayoclinic.org, www.statins.mercola.com, www.webmd.com* or *www.drugs.com* all have side effects and more listed. The FDA recently expanded their advice on statin risk to include; reports of memory loss, forgetfulness and confusion, risk of Type 2 diabetes, potential for muscle damage and liver injury. You can find this information on the FDA.gov web site under consumer updates. Yes, cholesterol needs to be at a normal healthy level. Levels too low are probably just as unhealthy as levels that are too high. Low levels of cholesterol can put your body at risk for developing oxidative stress. The unoxidized form of cholesterol has antioxidant properties to it and can protect cellular membranes from damage. This is all well known.

We need cholesterol to be healthy. Cholesterol is a steroid found in every cell of your body. It's in your plasma and it's an essential component of the structure of the cell membranes where it controls membrane fluidity. Cholesterol helps to produce cell membranes, hormones, vitamin D and the bile acids that help you digest fat. It is so important that I'm going to reiterate; cholesterol provides the structure of every steroid hormone in the body including adrenal and sex hormones. Also, the myelin sheaths of nerve fibers are derived from cholesterol and the bile salts that emulsify fats are composed of cholesterol.

According to neurologist David Perlmutter, MD and author of the book *Grain Brain,* "Your brain needs cholesterol to function. 25% of the cholesterol in your body is found in your brain where it plays important roles in such things as membrane function, acts as an antioxidant, and serves as the raw material from which we are able to make things like progesterone, estrogen, cortisol, testosterone and even vitamin D. In fact, in a recent study available on the NIH Public Access site,[19] researchers showed in the elderly, the best memory function was observed in those with the *highest* levels of cholesterol. Low cholesterol is associated with an increased risk for depression and even death." [20] Dr. Perlmutter is also a Fellow of the American Board of Nutrition.

It is well established that 60 – 80% of the body's cholesterol is synthesized by the liver, intestines and your skin, the rest comes from your diet. So I ask, "Is this a hormone we want to ignore by suppressing symptoms with a pill if the body is telling us something is going on? Or should we consider investigating why the cholesterol is elevated?"

I'm certainly not telling you to stop using your statin medication if you're taking statins. I am not a doctor. What I am saying is talk with your doctor before changing any medication and start getting curious as to why you have elevated cholesterol in the first place. If your doctor is unable to answer your questions or is unaware, maybe it's time to find a new doctor or a nutritionist who has been educated on the causes of cholesterol elevation. Whether or not you take a statin drug is up to you and your doctor. I am simply providing you a brief education about stress and cholesterol that I hope will peak your curiosity to research and educate yourself more.

Healing and restoration of normal function should be supported with a good nutritional program. When you choose healing, the idea is to restore and maintain balance, while correcting the inefficiencies in metabolic pathways. This means identifying and successfully reducing the stressors. Supporting adrenals is going to be important. One thing to note – when the body starts to clear out extra cholesterol, circulating cholesterol levels may temporarily elevate. This happened to me and with a little time my levels balanced out. I'm mentioning this because it is something to be aware of and from what I now understand is somewhat common. You will need the support of a qualified functional practitioner to monitor and guide you.

Identities and Stories

When people become ill or hurt in some way they may create a new identity. They take ownership of this new identity just as they do when they go from single life to the life of a couple, or change jobs and hold new or different titles. With these identities come our stories, our scripts. Once we adopt a script it can be very challenging to change it because we are probably not aware we are doing it.

If you had a parent who was not able to communicate very well and didn't express to you they were proud of your efforts and accomplishments, your view or perspective might be they didn't appreciate your efforts and accomplishments or your efforts and accomplishments were never 'enough'. As an adult you might go through your entire life replaying the script by putting yourself in situations where you work really hard but never get everything you set out to do accomplished, thereby continuing your childhood story of "I work really hard but it's never enough." You wonder why nobody appreciates you and it frustrates you to no end. The hardest part is seeing how you might be bringing these situations into your own life because it's part of your subconscious programming.

This was just a simple example many of us can relate to. So what does this have to do with healing from illness? It has everything to do with it! We have to get curious and figure out what scripts we are running. We have to become aware of our programming. Think about how a computer is programmed. It runs the same program over and over, good or bad until someone goes in and updates it. It's great when the programming functions well.

This may sound strange, but sometimes it can be frightening to heal. We may put a lot of pressure on ourselves, and wonder – what are people going to expect of me? Will I be able to measure up? Will I be able to do things I used to do? Will I fail? Who am I without the illness? Will people still show me love if I'm no longer ill? Do I deserve to be healthy and happy? When asking ourselves these questions without judgments we can get to the truth. The truth is literally what sets you free. By acknowledging and becoming aware of the patterns and scripts in your life, you can now be set free of them. You can make changes to the way you perceive and react, and this changes everything.

Look at how people "own" their illness. Listen to them talking about disease; they'll say "my _____ (the disease). If you have fibromyalgia, do you refer to it as your fibromyalgia? Do you really want to take ownership of it? Do you really want it to become a part of your identity? How would you be able to heal and let go of it if you do? Get curious about this without judgment. I'm not here to judge you. I have learned through my experience I had to let go of the identity of being sick in order to heal. I also had to let go of owning the disease in order to be able to let go of the identity.

The disease is a label describing a certain set of symptoms. Think of the symptoms as clues. We use the clues to try to pinpoint the imbalance so we can find opportunities for healing. Do you see how this goes? Wouldn't it be nice, if at all possible, to get to the root cause of an autoimmune or chronic disease? **How empowering would it be to have some understanding of what's going on in your body and be in a position to choose lifestyle changes to improve your health, instead of taking on the identity of the disease and fearing you are doomed with an illness that will rule your life forever?**

10
WHERE DOES NUTRITION COME FROM?

Healthy Soil, Healthy Plants, Healthy People.

If you start researching nutrition you will find there are thousands of articles showing a relationship between nutrition, diet, and health. There is more than enough literature connecting illness and disease with a lack of nutrition. Have you ever thought about where nutrition comes from? Most people will likely answer nutrition comes from a balanced diet. So, what is a balanced diet composed of? Food.

I've been aware of the link between nutritious food and healing for many years now. I have lived on farms most of my life. Growing much of my own nutrient rich food for close to 30 years was a necessity. I noticed simple things like the very low number of plant destroying insects in my garden and how sweet and wonderful the taste of my food was compared to food purchased at the grocery store. I connected the dots that mineral rich foods taste better and have a much longer shelf life! Without proper mineralization foods taste like cardboard and spoil much faster.

While some of my neighbors were busy buying and spraying chemicals in their gardens I pondered why insects were destroying the food in their gardens and not coming over and bothering mine. I began documenting my garden plants with photographs and showing the difference in food grown in nutrient rich, biologically abundant soils and food grown in poor soils. In addition to researching, I started attending courses and workshops through Acres USA, an organization that publishes a monthly magazine and promotes truly sustainable agriculture. The courses and workshops enabled me to better understand advanced soil science and why I was having success with what I was doing. I was able to learn from some of the best instructors in the world.

One of my favorite instructors is Arden Anderson, MD. I've attended several of his courses including his *Sustainable Agriculture – Advanced Systems for Eco-Farmers*. Arden was a soil consultant for about 10 years who then went to medical school. He understands health begins in the soil. He is one of the few people who really get it! He also understands and practices holistic medicine and holds a PhD in Public Health. When Dr. Anderson was teaching a class in 2007, he explained why the nutrient levels in food have declined so much. He said, "Agriculture has really dropped the ball relative to nutrition in the soil and then getting that nutrition into the plant, which is the food we eat. **Ultimately in order to change human health for the better, we have to go back and change the soil because that's where it (health) comes from. Preventive medicine begins in the soil.**" He went on to say according to his research, "the nutrient content of foods today compared to half a century ago ranges from 15-75% less. Food today is significantly deficient in nutrient density due to poor nutritional practices of farmers growing the food. This includes 'Organically Certified' food."

He continued to explain the decline began in the 1930's when farmers started using synthetic fertilizers known as the 'NPK model'. Other nutrients vital to plant and human health were neglected because they didn't seem to be needed to grow abundant crops. The original broader number of nutrients was never replenished and caused imbalance. Implemented solutions seem to have made things worse. According to Dr. Anderson many solutions were industry driven, particularly from World War II and on. Nitrates used for bomb making were being promoted and sold to farmers because nitrates promote very fast crop growth. He was specific about using nitrogen in agriculture because farmers got crop growth by volume. The problem with this option was the crops were not fit to eat. There was no nutritional value to speak of and that is one of the reasons why there has been a degradation of food.

He explained, "Nitrates are conducive to pathogens and harmful organisms. The same companies that have promoted the use of nitrogen are also manufacturing the pesticides to kill the organisms that are now going to be promoted by that fertilizer. It's a great business plan. It's not science at all, it's business." He concluded, "What you have to understand is every organism is dependent upon its environment. As we change the environment, we change which organisms will survive or perish.

As we change the nutrition in the soil and dynamics of what's going on in the soil, we can set up the appropriate environment for the beneficial microorganisms to survive, instead of the disease organisms. They do not like the same environment, particularly as it deals with oxygen. You will have an aerobic (oxygen-rich) environment versus an anaerobic (oxygen-deprived) environment. The beneficial organisms are predominately aerobic organisms. Pathogens, or harmful organisms, are predominately anaerobic. The environments that conventional agriculture has set up are predominately anaerobic environments, so they're mostly conducive to disease organisms."

Dr. Anderson also explained it this way in his presentation slide:

- "Diseases are environment dependent: nutrition determines who lives and dies."
- "Weeds are environment dependent: nutrition determines what microorganisms thrive which determines what plants thrive."
- "Insects are food dependent: they are designed to detect and locate food sources compatible with their digestive systems as does every other organism."
- "Truly healthy, mineralized plants do not get sick, do not rot, do not accumulate chemical toxins!"

"Environment determines genetic expression; regardless of the genes, it is the diet, nutrition and exogenous toxins to which one is exposed that determines health and disease. It's all about nutrition."

It made sense to me because you could have a room full of people exposed to a flu virus and not everyone will get it. Those that do get the flu may not have the exact same symptoms. Most doctors will agree it has something to do with the individual's immune system. Approximately 80% of our immune system is located in our gut. The gut environment determines the microorganisms which will thrive! Do you see where I'm going with this? I agree with Dr. Anderson that healthy mineralized plants don't get sick and do not rot. They also do not attract insects. That is my experience and what I have documented in my gardens. **Minerals are the building materials, microorganisms are the carpenters and without them there is no good health or life.**

This environment must include oxygen, water, food and comfort, the same things we humans need.

The way your food is grown really does matter, so hang in here with me for another minute and I'll try not to get too deep. If I do get a little deep it will only be for a moment. The environment in the soil determines which microorganisms will thrive, good or bad. In a supportive *soil* environment the microorganisms will feed the plant nutrients. In a supportive *gut* environment the microorganisms will feed you nutrients obtained from the plants. Do you see the similarities? What happens when a plant no longer has the proper nutrients available? It becomes attractive to insects. It is no longer a food that will support human health.

Francis Chaboussou, an agronomist of France's National Institute of Agricultural Research (INRA) presented a thesis titled *Trophobiosis*. He later wrote a book titled *Healthy Crops*, published in 1985, in which he lays out the science and the studies behind The Trophobiosis Theory. It is quite impressive and has given a deep understanding to how chemicals affect plant health, which affects human health. In his book he cites nearly 300 peer reviewed journal articles. The articles substantiate the fact that insects do not attack healthy plants, but only attack plants with an imbalance of nutrition, particularly with free nitrogen, amino acids and reducing sugars. Insects and pathogens seek soluble, free nutrients in a plant that is metabolically imbalanced due to inhibition of protein and complex carbohydrate synthesis. Chaboussou states, "...numerous organophosphates inhibit protein synthesis (in plants). This is the cause of the plant's increased susceptibility, not only to sucking insects,...but also to diseases, fungal and otherwise..."[21]

Chaboussou also said, "It seems that, in both animals and plants, susceptibility to disease is the result of metabolic problems." He continued, "It is no accident that, in exploring these issues of resistance and protection of the plant, we find ourselves face-to-face with the phenomenon of nutrition." [21]

If the plant receives the nutrition it needs it will be able to build complete proteins (protein synthesis). Complete proteins are what the human digestive system is designed to utilize. If a plant doesn't receive the full complement of nutrients needed it will not build complete proteins, this is called proteolysis. Where proteolysis dominates, disease thrives while the predominance of protein synthesis correlates with resistance to disease and insects.

"If your only tool is a chemical weapon everything will look like something to kill." – Dr. Arden Anderson

Insects have a digestive system designed to utilize incomplete proteins, the opposite (180 Degrees) of humans. As I said before, plants unable to complete protein synthesis become the perfect food for insects. Insects are God's garbage crew! Yes, there is a reason insects attack a plant. Insects attack only sick plants having incomplete proteins, free or fragmented nutrients, which insects are able to digest. "Plants that are not nutritious for the pests are also not palatable to them, the parasites will ignore them. Pests avoid healthy plants meant for human consumption."[21] I have witnessed this year after year in my garden and I have taught this concept to many Master Gardeners, back yard gardeners, and farmers successfully. If you would like to see some of the photos I use to demonstrate this in my powerpoint presentations, go to *www.cultivatinghealth.org*.

Today there is a massive problem with pest and disease in agriculture. Has this been brought on by the use of chemicals? If you read *Healthy Crops* or look at the studies presented in the book, you'll see some very strong indicators which point to that.

We are told chemical insecticides, fungicides, and herbicides are necessary. We hear all the time there are too many pests and diseases that must be killed. This 'war in the field' mentality is causing massive damage. Most chemicals used in agriculture are biocides; substances that harm living beings.[21] Francis Chaboussou and other scientists have shown how chemicals destroy microbes responsible for feeding nutrients to plants. These chemicals inhibit protein synthesis. This has led to an epidemic of plants and foods deficient in micro and macronutrients. This has led to an epidemic of sick plants and sick people. What affects soil and plants affects human health.

Dr. Anderson made clear during class every living organism has its required diet to be healthy and reproductive. He asked us if we would feed a pig's diet to a cow, a goat's diet to a pig, or an adult's diet to a baby. He explained insects, bacteria, fungi and viruses are no different. They do not have the digestive enzymes necessary to digest complete/complex proteins and carbohydrates (as humans do). They need simple sugars, amino acids and nitrogen compounds." The plant that has been sprayed with chemicals and is dominated by proteolysis provides that food.

We need to create a *180 Degree Wellness Revolution* on the farms growing our food. Think of the money we could save on healthcare if we could easily buy food that is free of chemicals and high in nutrition! The 'cost' of food is so much more than what you pay at the cash register. This is why it's important to buy quality food. Why would you want to spend hard earned money on low nutrient foods that hurt you? Spend a few cents more and purchase food which will support health. You are worth it.

What is the purpose of farming?

1. To produce food and fiber for human consumption, health and survival.
2. To provide complete nutrition.

3. To assist in recovery due to illness or trauma.

What can be done? We need to change the environment of our soils back to an aerobic environment so it is conducive to beneficial organisms rather than disease organisms. It's all about managing the biology. I tell people I am a soil farmer and practitioner! The soil is my client and my patient. I look at the history of the land. I go into the field or the garden and do a physical and visual exam, sometimes utilizing precision instruments and labs. I look for deficiencies in the soil. I examine the plants and their root systems. This will tell me what nutrients may be needed in order to change the environment. I almost always begin with calcium, since it is one of the most deficient nutrients in most soil and is necessary for utilization of other nutrients. Next, I bring in all of the trace minerals, not just a few of them. Carbohydrates would be next and so on. I use compost, humic acids, molasses, fish, seaweed, sea minerals and many other items to bring in the nutrients needed. If I manage the soil and the microbes, everything else works beautifully and growing food is easy.

Dr. Anderson expressed how agriculture, food, and medicine are intimately connected. It seems this purpose has been forgotten. Conventional Ag and their farmers don't seem to understand. Chemical weapons are toxic to human life and I don't know about you, but given a choice I certainly don't want to eat them on or in my food. Whatever is in the food, toxins or nutrients, directly determines the quality of life you and I have. Food is for nutrition, it is that simple. Vote with your dollars. Tell farmers you want quality food.

11
CREATING A PLAN TO GET STARTED

"The way to get started is to quit talking and start doing." – Walt Disney

First, I want to impress on you that simplicity is essential! Rebuilding and maintaining optimal function is not that complicated. Here it is:

- **Maximize:** Give your body the raw materials needed to heal and function. This may include protein, healthy fats, vitamins, minerals and antioxidants, and clean filtered water.
- **Minimize:** Remove what is harmful: stress, allergens, chemicals, toxins, infections, negative emotions and poor relationships.
- **Prioritize:** Create a healing environment for yourself. Enjoy nutrient rich food, play more, laugh more, create meaningful relationships, relax, sleep, reduce stress, rest and exercise.

The body will naturally seek wellness in a healing environment. People jump from one treatment protocol to another trying everything and then wonder why they aren't improving. The situation will not improve until you stop pouring gas on the fire. **You must address the reason the problem began in the first place.** This includes your personal habits. Otherwise you'll be destined to repeat, repeat, and repeat...undermining your own success! This will result in feelings of frustration and hopelessness. First, put out the fire and eliminate any smoldering.

Acknowledge what a damaging environment looks like and take steps to change your exposure. Keep it simple and don't overwhelm yourself. Simply replace one damaging habit or product each week with a healing habit or product (not too difficult) and within three months you will have changed twelve things. Change two things per week and in three months you'll have changed twenty-four. That's powerful!

Damaging Environment:

- Nutrient poor diet; **high** in processed foods, sugar, preservatives, chemical additives, hormone and drug laced animal foods and **low** in minerals and real foods like vegetables and fruit.
- Poor sleep habits, high stress, no time for fun.
- Toxin exposure consistent and constant; air, water, soil, food, dental, skin and hair products, makeup, drugs, household, playgrounds, lawn, heavy metals, etc.

There is no such thing as a pure lifestyle in the United States or most of the world, toxins are everywhere. This is why your liver is your best friend. Take care of it by removing and reducing whatever toxins you can and it will be better able to take care of you.

Building Your Support Team

I have to tell you, in my experience it has not been easy to find qualified practitioners who truly understand Functional Nutrition and Functional Medicine. You are likely to get very frustrated in your search at first because they are not on every street corner. Dr. Mark Hyman wrote an article that addresses this. The article is titled *Functional Medicine: How to Access the Future of Medicine Now*. You can find it on his blog dated May 2, 2013.[22] He writes about how hard it is to find a qualified practitioner who truly understands how to apply the Functional medical model. He says, "That's because it is a radically new way of thinking about health and disease, not just another treatment." He goes on to mention his introduction to Functional Medicine and some of his first patients at Canyon Ranch, "They were willing to spend time – often two hours – to see the nutritionist and get nutritional and metabolic testing that allowed me to see deep into the roots of their illness. And they were willing to make the lifestyle changes needed to address the causes of disease." Later in the article he states, "I want to emphasize – this is not alternative or integrative medicine, this is science-based, fundamental change in our way of thinking about health and disease."

It is not so much that it's radical and new; it's simply a departure from today's mainstream healthcare system. This "departure" brings us back around to the type of medicine practiced by doctors and veterinarians prior to the Industrial Revolution. Today, we have a lot more technology and tools too. Of course the doctors (and veterinarians) back then didn't have to contend with all of the chronic disease prevalent today due to lifestyle and poor diet issues. I really hope to see more and more practitioners learning the functional and nutritional model as Dr. Hyman has.

Finding a Functional Practitioner who looks at the whole body balance and is well versed in adrenals, thyroid, healing the gut and digestion is going to be important. This will be the foundation of your healing team. Having the right team will have a profound effect on your experience and give you the confidence to move forward.

Finding a Doctor or Practitioner

Research your local area first for practitioners educated in Funtional Nutrition. Below are three Internet sites I am aware of that have databases to help with a basic search. The databases contain many different kinds of practitioners, including Medical Doctor (MD), Doctor of Osteopathy (DO), Naturopathic Doctor (ND), Functional Diagnostic Nutrition®(FDN), Oriental Medical Doctor (OMD), Licensed Acupuncturist (L. Ac) and Homeopathic doctors. There might be other web sites with information on functionally trained practitioners that I'm unaware of. The key is to be specific in your search criteria. If you're unable to find someone local you can probably work long distance. (Skype and cell phones are making that easier these days.)

www.functionaldiagnosticnutrition.com - The Functional Diagnostic Nutrition web site lists practitioners who have been trained and certified in Functional Diagnostic Nutrition® (FDN) testing and protocols. Practitioners certified will have FDN after their name.

www.functionalmedicine.org - The institute for Functional Medicine web site lists practitioners who have attended an intensive 6-day training course.

www.acam.org - The American College for Advancement in Medicine web site has a directory that allows you to search for integrative practitioners. They may or may not be trained in Functional Medicine.

Other Support Team Members

- Health Coach/Counselor – A coach helps you to be accountable. They are becoming invaluable assets in solving lifestyle and diet challenges, as well as providing education for things like weight loss and preventive health and healing.
- Family and loved ones – Family members and loved ones need to understand the importance of the changes you are making for your health and longevity. This is not always an easy task. They may not be comfortable with change and could see what you're dong as a threat to them. You may get accused of overdoing it or being too picky. Everything you do affects them in some way too. There will likely be changes in meal planning and restaurants you choose to frequent, which could affect the spouse and kids. If you go to a friend's home for dinner you might want to start bringing a main dish or soup so you never have to worry about what is being served and you can enjoy dinner regardless of what others are eating. This is especially true if you are gluten free.

I remember when my daughter was in second grade. I always made fresh real-food lunches for her to take to school. She loved those lunches until one day she told me her friends thought her food was yucky! I asked her if they had tasted her food, she replied no, and we laughed because how could they know it's yucky if they had never tasted it. One day when her friends were over at our house I offered them some fresh canteloupe out of the garden, they immediately refused saying they didn't like cantaloupe, it tastes like cardboard. I assured them it wasn't like the cantaloupe from the store they said tastes like cardboard, so they agreed to try it. They loved it and said it was like candy. From that day on there was always a big bowl of fresh fruit devoured when they came over and I sometimes sent extra to school so she could share her yummy food with her friends.

Family and friends can be really supportive if they have an opportunity to understand and even share in the fun of discovering new foods. People seem to automatically think healthy food doesn't taste good and that is not true. It is actually just the opposite... a 180 Degree difference! **Healthy foods taste so much better than processed food and leave you feeling satiated and content.** Take the time necessary and offer opportunities which may help them to welcome your changes instead of fearing them. If they can be supportive, your stress will be lowered. Always remember though, you can't force anyone to do anything they don't want to do. Fear of change is a big hurdle and it may take a while to get through. So, do what you need to do for yourself and as family and friends notice you feeling and looking better they may get curious and let go of the fear.

Prepare Yourself

Unfortunately, insurance is not going to pay for many of the necessities required to regain health and prevent disease. You will need to make an investment in yourself. That was a tough one for me because money was tight due to illness. I eventually saw I was worth the investment and found ways to reduce spending and 'do without' in certain areas to allow myself the testing and care I needed. It has paid off more than I ever thought possible.

Next, you will need to remember if you are dealing with chronic illness or an autoimmune condition you are going to learn again and again the definition of patience. There is no overnight fix with a pill – none that I'm aware of. Chronic illness develops over a long period of time and it may take awhile to rebuild your health and turn it around (do the 180!). Are you willing to do this? Be patient and loving towards yourself. Make yourself a promise you will become the most patient person on your team! In addition, it will be very important to look honestly at your commitment level. People who are only partially committed will not succeed. You must be committed to building health, get real with yourself about that. If you are not fully committed ask yourself, "What is preventing me from being fully committed?" and "What needs to change?" Maybe it's the belief you'll never be able to do it or you don't have enough time. Whatever it is, address it honestly by asking yourself, "Is that really the truth?" **The only person who can build your health is YOU.** Your practitioner is simply the guide on the side. When you are committed, you are ready.

Some things you will need to look at:

1. What foods are you eating? What are the ingredients of these foods?
2. What effect do the foods have on your unique body? Are you addicted to any foods?
3. Do you have food sensitivities?
4. How is your digestion? Your pH?
5. Is your level of stomach acid too low?
6. Do you crave certain foods or drinks? What are they?
7. Are you absorbing nutrients?
8. How are your hormones?
9. What does your poop look like? (Yes, you have to look at your poop!)
10. What are your stressors?
11. Are you taking time to nurture yourself?

12. What is your body trying to tell you?

Your perspective on food may need to do a 180. Look at food and proper supplementation as a chance to heal and maintain function. Stay away from foods that have more than **five simple ingredients**. If you can't pronounce an ingredient, don't eat it. Preferably eat foods grown organically that don't have ingredient labels! Eat the foods your great grandmother would have grown up eating. It really is that simple.

Labs and Testing

You may never need to know much about the following tests, but your practitioner should be aware of them and have resources available if they are ever needed, to correctly interpret results. ***(I want to make a note that these tests are not conclusive; there are many different tests available on the market and these are simply the ones that I am most familiar with.)*** Testing you may want to be aware of:

- **CDSA 2.0** – The Comprehensive Digestive Stool Analysis 2.0™. This test looks at the overall health of the gastrointestinal tract. Helps to evaluate digestion, absorption, inflammation, bacterial balance, yeast and parasite infection.
- **IgG Food Sensitivity Panel** – Looks for chronic inflammatory response. A very useful guide in structuring elimination diets for many chronic conditions.
- **Comprehensive Thyroid Panel** – Excellent thyroid function and thyroid autoimmune (Hashimoto's) test. Should include TSH (Thyroid Stimulating Hormone), TSH free, T4 (Thyroxin) total, T4 free, T3 (triiodothyronine) total, T3 free, T3 uptake, T3 reverse, both TgAB (Thyroglobulin auto-antibodies), TPOAb (Thyroid

peroxidase auto-antibodies).

- **4 Sample Cortisol Saliva Assessment** – Tests multiple saliva samples taken at specific times of the day to allow real-time evaluation of hormonal stress response and circadian rhythm. Easily collected by the patient at work or home.
- **CBC Blood Panel with Hormones and Inflammatory Markers** – Complete Blood Count Panel with Differential and Platelets. Chemistry/Metabolic Panel measures your homeostatic markers and organ function. Lipid panel measures cholesterol and fats. Hormone Panel for males will include Estradiol (E2), LH, Testosterone, Free Testosterone, DHT, DHEA-S, Cortisol, PSA. Hormone Panel for females includes Estradiol (E2), Progesterone, LH, FSH, Testosterone, DHEA-S, Cortisol. Growth Hormone Markers include IGF-1 and IGFBP-3. Inflammation Marker Panel should include Sedimentation rate, Cardiac CRP and Homocysteine.
- **Organic Acids Test** – Nutritional and metabolic profile looks for markers in urine sample for evaluation of intestinal micro-organisms such as yeast and bacteria.
- **Intestinal Permeability Assessment** – A non-invasive assessment of small intestinal absorption and barrier function in the bowel. Urine sample test.
- **SIBO Breathing Test** – Small Intestinal Bacteria Overgrowth. Breath test measures the Hydrogen (H) & Methane (M) gas produced by bacteria in the small intestine that has diffused into the blood, then lungs for expiration. H & M are gases produced by bacteria, not humans.

- **Celiac Panel** – Blood test that screens for celiac disease antibodies. You must be eating gluten for this antibody testing to be accurate. Most common test is tTG-IgA test. Also used is IgA Endomysial antibody (EMA), Total serum IgA, and Deaminated gliadin peptide (DGP IgA and IgG). There is also genetic testing available.
- **MTHFR Mutation/Methylation** – This test checks for a mutation in the MTHFR gene and enzyme which helps regulate homocysteine levels, process folate, optimize Methylation and much more in the body. This may be key information for those whom have trouble detoxing.

Just because a lab value is within the 'reference range' does not mean it is necessarily fine and shouldn't be looked at further. Lab reference ranges are based on an average. This average is based on the people who are being tested. When do people usually get their blood tested? Many times it's when they're not feeling well. How many of these people are dealing with health issues and on medications? How does this affect the average lab reference range? Testing can show you what is going on now and it can show you where things have been or are trending towards. Let's use blood sugar for example. If you received "normal" results for fasting blood sugar for the last three years that would mean your blood sugar fell within the typical reference range of 80-100 mg/dl. Your doctor's office may call or send you a note saying everything's normal. Just a few years ago the 'normal' range was 90-120; your doctor would have given you the same 'everything's normal' response. But is it? If you take a moment and compare the current lab report to previous lab reports, you may notice some very important information. The labs show each year the numbers increased; (2010 90mg/dl, 2011 95mg/dl, 2012 100mg/dl). Could this be an opportunity to identify a trending pattern and learn you may be progressing towards insulin resistance? Is this the prime time, while it is sub-clinical to make lifestyle or diet changes to prevent the possible future clinical diagnoses of diabetes? I suggest working with a practitioner who understands this concept.

My husband worked in public safety for 31 years. Each year he was given a physical and was required to pass to be fit for duty. The doctors would find occasional lab values slightly outside of the 'normal' range. The common interpretation was "He was still young, nothing to worry about." I disagreed and debated him on this for years! My husband liked the doctor saying there was nothing to worry about. If you ask me, the doctor should have been saying "You're still young, make the necessary changes before irreversible harm is done." Now my husband sees very clearly how misguided it was.

12
PREPARATION OF THE MIND
A PARADIGM SHIFT

Conscious choice to heal and not continue the toxic overload reduces your risk of participating in creating illness.

Actions speak louder than words. People are creatures of habit and not always willing to do the basic things required to bring about change. We naturally want to keep the same habits even though those habits may have created a detrimental situation. We may say we want to change, but our actions don't reflect our words and we may not even realize we're doing this. There is a thought process necessary for an individual to be open, which will allow transformation necessary for healing.

In order to overcome self-sabotage patterns learned as a child, a person must open their mind, realize they are resisting something, and let go of resistance. It's kind of like when I go out into my garden and get ready to plant in the spring, I have to loosen and prepare the soil so the seed has an environment in which it can sprout and grow successfully. If the soil environment is too tight, too dry, or not supportive of the seed, then the seed will not continue to live and grow into a thriving plant. For any of it to work I have to evaluate and notice the condition of the soil first. So, try to evaluate and notice the condition of your mind. Is it closed up tightly? Do you find yourself being defensive a lot? Are you making decisions based on fear? Is there a fear of being rejected, fear of change, fear you've been lied to? Just notice without judgment and you can learn a great deal about yourself. Be willing to admit maybe you need to loosen up the 'soil' of your mind.

In order to heal, one must observe their beliefs. I'm not talking about religion. I'm talking about beliefs you were taught while growing up. These are the scripts and stories in your mind about who you are and what you are capable of. **Revising beliefs and stories where needed can change your life dramatically. It impacts your behavior, your expectations, your reactions, and how you do things in every way.** This action of rewriting beliefs is essential to healing work and is not about blame or shame. It is about learning what you've been taught throughout life and understanding how it directly affects you today. There is so much we are unaware of and so often we just don't know what we don't know. Opening up to see where our behavior patterns come from and learning how to shift beliefs will allow healing to happen in a much easier way. We can easily sabotage ourselves due to the beliefs we carry within us.

It's very important to understand and learn to live the concept of believing in yourself because when you believe you are fully capable of something, you now open an opportunity to enjoy the benefits of that capability. If you don't believe you are capable, you will never have an opportunity to enjoy the benefits, which may come if you did believe. In other words, if you don't believe you can possibly heal, you won't be able to allow healing in your life. **Believing is the first step to anything. If you don't believe it can happen, it won't! It's that simple.** If the Wright brothers hadn't believed they could build an airplane and fly, how would things be different today? People thought they were nuts, but the Wright brothers didn't listen to what others believed. They understood on some level that those who told them they couldn't fly simply didn't know what they knew. The Wright brothers believed they could fly an airplane and they did.

I was told I had irreversible autoimmune thyroid disease and at first I believed I would never be able to reverse it. I also believed at one point I was going to have to rely on a wheelchair for whatever days remained. All of the hope I held on to had been stripped from me because of the words of a few people. I began questioning how doctors and research papers came to such conclusions, as if they were psychic. Do they really know what the rest of my life is going to be like? I gave myself permission to reconsider their words and to **stop believing** what I had been told my life was going to look like. I would think back to my near death experience and realize that maybe they don't know what they don't know. Our medical system really breeds dependency and I asked myself why. Why do some doctors believe a person cannot get better or needs to take a pill for every ailment while others do not? I don't know the answer; maybe in some way it's tied to belief systems and the need to feel needed. I began shifting my beliefs and that is when my healing began. Never, is a huge word that is no longer in my vocabulary!

So many amazing accomplishments on this planet wouldn't have happened if people hadn't believed they were possible. When we start a process, such as healing an illness and we don't believe we can do it, we inherently fill ourselves with doubt and set ourselves up to never achieve the outcome. **You have to believe you can do it!** If you don't, you need to look at why you believe what you believe. Einstein said, "We can't solve problems by using the same kind of thinking we used when we created them."

It's time to realize you innately know more about your own body than anyone else. You have an inner pilot light; your intuition. Your intuition can help guide you if you learn to trust it. It took me a while to trust my own instincts because of things that occurred in my life when I was much younger. I can tell you today; I always listen to my intuition and trust it 100% . I took matters into my own hands, educated myself on true healing, and what is called alternative medicine (I call it advanced medicine). I gave myself permission to take charge and to not hand over my power to others, including a doctor.

As my friend Dr. Robert Scott Bell says, **"The Power to Heal is yours."**

For more information on upcoming group programs, speaking events, photos related to this book, or if you would like to hire Tara to speak at your upcoming event, please visit the authors web sites at: www.180DegreeWellnessRevolution.com and *www.CultivatingHealth.org.*

****

I am so proud to be a graduate of the Institute for Integrative Nutrition®. If you would like to learn more about this ground-breaking school and community, go to the *Integrativenutrition.com* website or call (877) 730-5444. IIN® offers a special (significant!) tuition discount to my readers. Just mention Tara L. Gesling or copy this web address into your browser to get more information - *http://goo.gl/zbtdpo.*

BIBLIOGRAPHY

[1] *Ignaz Semmelweis - Wikipedia*. (n.d.). Retrieved September 9, 2014, from Wikipedia.org: http://en.wikipedia.org/wiki/Ignaz_Semmelweis

[2] *Ignaz Semmelweis - Wikipedia*. (n.d.). Retrieved September 9, 2014, from Wikipedia.org: http://en.wikipedia.org/wiki/Ignaz_Semmelweis#Efforts_to_reduce_childbed_fever

[3] Agency, U. E. (n.d.). *Mercury*. Retrieved September 9, 2014, from EPA.gov: http://www.epa.gov/hg/dentalamalgam.html

[4] Mercola, D. (2010, October 9). *Mercola.com archive 2010/10/09*. Retrieved September 9, 2014, from Mercola.com: http://articles.mercola.com/sites/articles/archive/2010/10/09/jeff-smith-interview-gmo-week.aspx

[5] Technology, A. I. (2013, December 20). *GMO Health Dangers Spilling the Beans Newsletter*. Retrieved September 1, 2014, from Responsible Technology.org: http://www.responsibletechnology.org/posts/gmo-health-dangers/

[6] Technology, A. -I. (n.d.). *Institute for Responsible Technology - FAQ's*. Retrieved August 17, 2014, from IRT - The Institute For Responsible Technology: www.responsibletechnology.org/faqs

[7] Huff, E. A. (2014, August 8). *Natural News*. Retrieved August 20, 2014, from Natural News.com: http://www.naturalnews.com/046370_organic_food_antioxidants_pesticides.html

[8] University, N. (2014, July 11). *Newcastle University Press Office*. Retrieved August 10, 2014, from Newcastle University: http://www.ncl.ac.uk/press.office/press.release/item/new-study-finds-significant-differences-between-organic-and-non-organic-food

[9] Zerbe, L. (n.d.). *Rodale News - The Truth About Organic*. Retrieved August 14, 2014, from Rodalenews.com: http://www.rodalenews.com/organic-foods-study

[10] Institute, R. (2012). *Rodale Institute Farming Systems Trial*. Retrieved August 1, 2014, from Rodale Institute: http://rodaleinstitute.org/our-work/farming-systems-trial/

[11] Mercola, D. (2009, April 25). *Mercola.com - Irradiated Food Causes Brain Damage.* Retrieved July 5, 2014, from www.mercola.com: http://articles.mercola.com/sites/articles/archive/2009/04/25/Irradiated-Food-Causes-Brain-Damage.aspx

[12] Duncan, D. o. (2009, April 21). *Pubmed.gov.* Retrieved July 5, 2014, from Pubmed - National Institutes of Health: http://www.ncbi.nlm.nih.gov/pubmed/19342494

[13] Meyers, D. A. (2013, September 12). Retrieved July 14, 2014, from http://www.mindbodygreen.com/0-10908/9-signs-you-have-a-leaky-gut.html

[14] Buttar, D. (2014, August 11). Medical Rewind. (R. S. Bell, Interviewer). http://www.medicalrewind.com/prevention-of-cancer-formaldehyde-is-a-carcinogen-what-is-the-cure-for-cancer/

[15] Laboratory, G. P. (n.d.). *Oxalates - Test Implications for Yeast & Heavy Metals*. Retrieved August 12, 2014, from The Great Plains Laboratory, Inc: www.greatplainslaboratory.com/home/eng/oxalates.asp

[16] Shaw, D. W. (n.d.). *The Great Plains Laboratory Oxalates*. Retrieved August 5, 2014, from Great Plains Laboratory: http://www.greatplainslaboratory.com/home/eng/oxalates.asp

[17] Amino, N. (2007, March 7). *4 Autoimmunity and hypothyroidism - Summary*. Retrieved August 20, 2014, from ScienceDirect: http://www.sciencedirect.com/science/article/pii/S0950351X88800557

[18] Mercola, D. (2010, July 20). *Mercola.com archive* . Retrieved August 12, 2014, from Mercola.com: http://articles.mercola.com/sites/articles/archive/2010/07/20/the-truth-about-statin-drugs-revealed.aspx

[19] Mt Sinia School of Medicine, N. (2008, September 16). *PubMed.* Retrieved August 16, 2014, from PubMed.gov: http://www.ncbi.nlm.nih.gov/pubmed/18757771

[20] Perlmutter, D. (n.d.). *David Perlmutter MD Your Brain Needs Cholesterol*. Retrieved September 2, 2014, from www.Drperlmutter.com: http://www.drperlmutter.com/brain-needs-cholesterol/

[21] Chaboussou, F. (2004). *Healthy Crops A New Agricultural Revolution.* England: John Carpenter Publishing.

[22] Hyman, D. M. (2013, May 2). *Functional Medicine: How to Access the Future of Medicine Now*. Retrieved July 12, 2014, from Drhyman.com: http://drhyman.com/blog/2010/08/08/functional-medicine-how-to-access-the-future-of-medicine-now/

NOTES

Made in the USA
San Bernardino,
CA